Who is John Blanke?

Michael I. Ohajuru holds an Honorary Doctorate from the Open University (2024), is a Fellow of the Royal Society of Arts (2022), Senior Fellow of the Institute of Commonwealth Studies (2014), with honours degrees in Physics (Leeds, 1974) and Art History (Open University, 2008). He retired in 2014 after a 25-year career holding senior positions in international sales and marketing in the data and mobile communications industry. He lives in South London with his partner, the artist Ebun Culwin.

He blogs, writes and speaks regularly on the Black presence in Renaissance Europe, he has spoken at the Metropolitan Museum, New York, the National Gallery, London, National Portrait Gallery, Tate Britain, British Library, National Archives and the Victoria Albert Museum and has been invited to speak at Yale University on the subject.

In 2010, he founded Image of the Black in London Galleries – a series of gallery tours highlighting the overt and covert Black presences to be found in the national art collections in London.

He is Project Director and Chief Evangelist of the John Blanke Project, a contemporary Art and Archive project celebrating John Blanke, the Black trumpeter to the courts of Henry VII and Henry VII now in the permanent collection of the National Portrait Gallery. He is a co-convenor of What's Happening in Black British History?, a series of workshops fostering creative dialogue between researchers, educationalists (mainstream and supplementary), archivists and curators, and policymakers; a series of 10 workshops were held over five years.

He is a founder member of the Black Presence in British BP2 Podcast.

Michael I. Ohajuru DUniv, FRSA
Art and Cultural Historian
https://about.me/michaelohajuru/

Photo by David VY Wallis

Who is John Blanke?

Historians and Artists Reimagine the Black Tudor Trumpeter

**Edited by
Michael I. Ohajuru**

First published by Canbury Press 2025
This edition published 2025

 Canbury Press (www.canburypress.com)
14 Beresford Road, Kingston upon Thames, United Kingdom
www.canburypress.com

EU Authorised Representative: Easy Access System Europe - Mustamäe tee 50, 10621 Tallinn, Estonia, gpsr.requests@easproject.com

Printed and bound in Czechia by Finidr

Designed by James Alexander at Jade Design
Typeset in Salford Sans (designed by Lewis McGuffie/David Williams/Elsa Baussier) & Garamond Premier Pro

All rights reserved © Michael I. Ohajuru 2024

Michael I. Ohajuru has asserted his right to be identified as the author of this work in accordance with Section 77 of the Copyright, Designs and Patents Act 1988

All the works, except for that by Bob and Roberta Smith, are privately owned by the John Blanke Project

This is a work of non-fiction

Hardback ISBN 978 19 14487 48 4
Ebook ISBN 978 19 14487 49 1

Supported by a Publications Grant from the Paul Mellon Centre for Studies in British Art

Where history loses form, art and poetry take shape

Alexandre White, Asst Professor, Johns Hopkins University

It's good to see your face

Eva Martindale-Ohajuru (1928-2016)

Dedicated to my grandchildren
Jessica, Sebastian and Cian

Foreword 8

Introduction 9

The John Blanke Project 10

The Great Tournament Roll of Westminster 18

Artists and Historians 21

Artificial Intelligence and the John Blanke Project 258

Sources 259

Recommended Reading 261

John Blanke Live! 262

The John Blanke Project Timeline 264

Crowdfunder Thanks 265

Acknowledgements 266

Corporate and Institution Thanks 267

The John Blanke Project in Videos and Podcasts 268

Contributors 269

Foreword

John Blanke the Blacke Trumpet

His name is on what we would call a payment slip.

For services rendered.

This is how we know the name of this Black Tudor musician, one of the few Black people from that time that we can name.

I had always only seen reproductions of his image.

Until the former Director of the British Museum, Hartwig Fischer, got Michael, me and colleagues into the College of Arms.

There we saw one of their most prized objects: *The Westminster Tournament Roll of 1511*, created to celebrate the festivities in honour of the birth of the son of Henry VIII and his queen, Catherine Of Aragon.

The tournament roll is made of vellum-sheepskin and can only rarely be taken out and shown.

It's a 500 plus year old document, it needs careful conservation to stay in good condition.

The sheer joy of standing there with Michael as the tournament roll was unfolded – slowly and gently – made us both sing spontaneously that great Motown classic:

'Ain't Nothin' Like The Real Thing.'

Because there isn't.

John Blanke. There before us. The real thing.

What I thought when I looked at him was how the makers of the tournament roll must have been in awe of him.

The detail: his cap; his eyes; the colour of his skin.

So carefully rendered, a tribute to this trumpeter of the King.

John Blanke – Human Being here; A Man like any other.

And yet: bold and confident enough to seek his due in a world unafraid of him.

Beautiful and noble, too, sitting astride his horse, working his trumpet in proclamation of a future king.

I am so very grateful to Michael Ohajuru and to his The John Blanke Project.

I am grateful for his rigorous research and his relentless championing of this Black Tudor man.

The study and celebration of him – along with Michael's work – should be one of the cornerstones of British education.

I mean this.

The history of Black people here in the UK is long and deep and wide and high, and glorious, noble.

And beautiful.

All hail John Blanke and The John Blanke Project!

Dr Bonnie Greer OBE FRSL
Former Deputy Chair, British Museum

Introduction

The John Blanke Project originated in 2013 from a shared passion for uncovering and exploring the Black presence in Tudor England. Its foundation was laid during a series of talks titled *Image and Reality: Black Africans in Renaissance England (IRBARE)*, a collaboration between Dr Miranda Kaufmann and the project's founder, Michael. These talks juxtaposed the depiction of Black figures in art, such as the Black Magus, with historical evidence of real Black individuals in England, such as John Blanke, the Black trumpeter to the courts of Henry VII and Henry VIII.

John Blanke holds a unique place in British history as the first known person of African descent for whom we have both an image and documented records. Despite his fleeting presence in Tudor records, his significance is undeniable. Two depictions of Blanke appear in the Great Tournament Roll of Westminster, and archival documents record his wages, his petition for a pay increase, and gifts from Henry VIII. The project aims to reimagine his life and legacy, transforming his ephemeral history into a vibrant narrative through art and scholarship.

The commissioning process is central to the project's purpose. Artists and historians are invited to imagine John Blanke's life and role at court. The initial inspiration came from artist Stephen B. Whatley's mural featuring John Blanke at Tower Hill. Whatley's depiction prompted the founder to commission other artists to create A4 black-and-white works interpreting John Blanke. These works are accompanied by a statement beginning, "I imagined John Blanke as…" The artists' statements are online at JohnBlanke.com all their images are seen togther for the first time here.

In parallel, historians contribute essays exploring various aspects of Blanke's life and significance. The historians' contributions are on line in full at JohnBlanke.com. Together, these artistic and scholarly contributions create a multidisciplinary celebration of John Blanke, challenging assumptions about the Black presence in Tudor England and fostering a more inclusive understanding of British history.

John Blanke.com

The John Blanke Project: Exploring the Black Tudor Trumpeter through Art and History

The John Blanke Project

First printed as 'Before and After the Eighteenth Century: The John Blanke Project' in Britain's Black Past: New Writings on Britain's Black Past, Liverpool, Liverpool University Press (2020)

Updated by the Author in November 2024

Introduction

My book, *Who is John Blanke? Historian and Artist Reimagine the Black Tudor Trumpeter*, takes its title from the very first question I was asked when introducing this remarkable historical figure. Over a decade ago, John Blanke and his fellow Black Tudors were virtually unknown. Today, much has changed. John Blanke has become a Tudor 'poster boy,' featured on book and magazine covers, brought to life in radio plays and TV history dramas, and even making a cameo appearance in *Wolf Hall*.
To explore his story, I commissioned artists and historians to answer that very question — Who is John Blanke?— through their creative imaginations. By drawing from his brief but significant appearances in Tudor records and the two surviving images of him, they have brought him to life in ways that blend history and imagination. My John Blanke Project is more than a rediscovery; it is a celebration of John Blanke's legacy, illustrating how Black British history connects past and present. *Who is John Blanke?* is both a question and an invitation – one that continues to inspire new interpretations and reflections on his life and times.

John Blanke, the Black trumpeter to the Tudor court, is the first person of African descent for whom we have both an identifiable image and documentation. He makes a number of brief appearances in court records between 1495 and 1512. His fleeting presence in those records invites many questions: Was that his real name? Where did he come from? Whom did he marry? Where did he go after leaving Henry's court? The John Blanke Project asks contributors to address such questions as they imagine the Black Tudor trumpeter, inviting them to respond in their chosen media. There are 114 contributions, including work from historians, visual artists, poets, photographers, rappers, musicians, and playwrights. The project, with its strapline *Imagine the Black Tudor Trumpeter*, encourages imaginative and creative thought about the Black presence – not just in Tudor history but in British history as a whole.

Background to the Project

The inspiration for the Project came from two sources. First, a series of presentations I gave in 2013 with Dr Miranda Kaufmann, These presentations were based on a shared interest in the Black presence in 15th and 16th century Europe in general and England in particular. Second, the work of the visual artist Stephen B Whately. The presentations Dr Kaufmann and I gave were entitled *Image and Reality: Black Africans in Renaissance England* (IRBARE). I reviewed images of the Black by artists from the period, while Dr Kaufmann presented the results of her doctoral research. Stephen was commissioned in 1999 to create a series of paintings on the history of the Tower of London and The Pool of London, in which he included a small image of John Blanke as a marginal, supporting figure. The Black trumpeter can be found in the painting showing Henry VIII jousting before his queen, Katherine of Aragon – one of the series of 30 paintings Stephen produced to complete the commission. Together, IRBARE and Stephen's image were the stimulus for the John Blanke Project.

In IRBARE, Dr Kaufmann introduced the audience to the lives of some of the 360-plus sub-Saharan African men, women and children she had found living in England and Scotland in the period. Her evidence came from parish registers, church accounts, tax returns, household accounts, wills, diaries, letters and other documents. She found them living all over the UK, from Aberdeen to Truro. The references were most times quite fleeting; some might say simply buried with a date, lost amongst so many other similar written records. For example, in the burial records of St Martin in the Fields for the year 1571, most deaths are recorded as a single line. In September that year, eight deaths are recorded and seven have just the name of the deceased. The entry for the burial on the 27th of that month includes not just the name 'Margureta', however, but also the note '... A Moore', from which Dr Kaufmann deduced she was both a Christian and Black. Dr Kaufmann's evidence for the Black African presence in the Tudor period came almost entirely from equally brief, contemporaneous written records, from which she was able to piece together their lives. She could see what work they did, where and whom they married and generally how they survived and – in some cases – thrived.

John Blanke was the one exception, pictured twice in the Great Tournament Roll of Westminster and mentioned in the court accounts of Henry VII and Henry VIII. For the court musician, there was not just a written record, but also an image.
While Dr Kaufmann had just two images of a known Black African from the period to discuss, I had many hundreds, as the Black Magus or King in the biblical adoration image was an established figure in European religious art, which dated back to the thirteenth century. The Black figure, as part of the adoration scene, was to be found throughout Europe during the period, including England. The image of the Black King would have been well known and understood at that time , despite the fact that no African King visited Europe during the period. The figure of the Black King, along with much of the Adoration scene itself, was a conflation, interpretation and presentation of biblical study, courtly practice and artistic tradition. He never actually existed. I discussed the image of the Black King, what it meant religiously, socially, and what it signified. His presence followed several established conventions: his position, his clothing, his stance and his gold earring all acting as signifiers of 'the other' or 'not one of us'. In the process, a composition was created of one king and two kings – one Black and two white – rather than three kings.

It can be argued that this difference was perhaps how one of the definitions of whiteness, as a differentiator from Black, crystallised in Renaissance Europe at a time when Black Africans were considered culturally to be barbarians and legally slaves. IRBARE made problematic contrasts between the image and reality of Black Africans. On the one hand, we have the actual lived reality of Black Africans as common, ordinary people – making a living in society as discovered from the archives. On the other, we see the fabricated image of the Black African as part of an elite – a king depicted in one of the key images of the Christian Gospel, in which earthly kings pay homage to Jesus, the king of both Heaven and Earth. That image was to be found in churches throughout Europe. The contrast was emphasised by Dr Kaufmann's two images of a real Black African on the Great Tournament Roll of Westminster from the period – John Blanke – and the many hundreds of images of the Black King I had to call upon, even though he never actually existed, underling the disparity between image and the reality of Black Africans at that time.

Through my work with IRBARE, I became aware of Stephen B. Whatley's monumental work on permanent display at Tower Hill tube station, where his paintings had been reproduced in a series of panels lining the walls of the underpass from the tube station to the Tower of London, centred on the life and times of Henry VIII. Stephen took as his sources original historic documents, including the Great Tournament Roll of Westminster from the College of Arms. He took that document's central scene (Henry VIII jousting before his queen and the ladies of the court, completing one of the highest scoring 'tilts') from the Tournament Roll. Surviving score cards from the joust reveal that, although the King was quite successful, that score was never actually achieved. The image is artistic licence, flattering the King.

Stephen produces a stylised, modernist version of the scene in his distinctive individual, idiosyncratic, colour palette of pastel greens, blues, pinks, reds and yellows, which wash into each other in his oil paintings like water colours. They create soft, muted edges between coloured forms in which he recreates the drama and movement of Henry's jousting before his Queen. On the edge of Stephen's painting are the trumpeters, including John Blanke. We know it is John, as Stephen differentiates him by his facial colouring and a turban. The Black musician was the only one of the troop of six trumpeters to wear any head covering and, as a consequence, his presence as depicted by Stephen is very distinctive.

I have had the opportunity to discuss with Stephen his depiction of John Blanke and, to my surprise, he was not looking to make any statements on the Black presence in Tudor times. He simply wanted to make an interesting composition based on the Tournament Roll. John Blanke's ethnicity did not preoccupy him at all in the way that it preoccupied me. I liked Stephen's work so much I commissioned him to produce an A5 drawing of John

Figure 1. Stephen B. Whatley, *Tribute to John Blanke*, (2015), charcoal on paper, A4

Blanke from his Tower of London work, although he generously produced an A4 piece (figure 1).

It is a modernist drawing, in which Stephen has captured the sound and movement of John Blanke from the Great Tournament Roll of Westminster as a black-and-white image. Stephen's work made me reflect on IRBARE, where there were just two images of John Blanke in that one document, now believed to be the only portrayal of a known Black African in Britain the period. This contrasted with the many hundreds, perhaps thousands, of images of the Black King I have seen – despite the fact that John Blanke was real and that the Black King was a fabricated conflation. It occurred to me I might commission other artists to produce their imagined versions of John Blanke, based on his image and record from the archives, with a view to holding an exhibition of them along with the original image from the Tournament Roll. Thus, began The John Blanke Project

History of the John Blanke Image

John Blanke's image lay ignored, forgotten in the archives from the courts of Henry VII and Henry VIII for almost half a millennium. It has taken the detailed, persistent work of dedicated academic and community historians to bring John Blanke and his image to life. It was not until the mid 1950s that he was first revived. This resurrection was brought about by the diligent, systematic work of Dr Sydney Anglo, who, at the time, was doing postdoctoral research on early Tudor court festivals. At the National Archives, working through the account books of John Heron, Treasurer of the Chamber, Dr Anglo examined records covering the reigns of Henry VII and Henry VIII. There, under December 7th 1507, was the record that John Blanke was paid eight pennies (viiid) a day, 20 shillings (xxs) for the month. This was the first of several payments to John Blanke 'the blacke trumpet'.

> *Item to John Blanke, the blacke trumpet for his month wages of Novembre last passed at viijd the day........xxs*

At the same time, Dr. Anglo was studying manuscripts at the College of Arms, one of which was the Great Tournament Roll of Westminster, where he found two representations of a 'blacke trumpet', at the centre-rear of a troop of six trumpeters on horseback in two rows of three. He made the connection between 'the blacke trumpet' in the two documents – John Blanke in John Heron's accounts was the Black trumpeter in the Tournament Roll. Dr Anglo re-introduced John Blanke to the modern world within a footnote to this analysis of John Heron's accounts :

> *I believe this John Blank [sic] was, in fact, a Negro in the Great Roll of the Tournament at Westminster in February 1511, preserved at the College of Arms, a negro musician is twice depicted amongst the king's trumpets. This I think was John Blank [sic], the 'blacke trumpet'.*

John Blanke might have remained a footnote only known and easily available to academics if not for the work of Audrey Dewjee and Ziggi Alexander, who brought the court musician to life for a second time. On this occasion, it would be for a wider non-academic and community audience.

In early 1980, they went to an exhibition of heraldry at the British Museum in an attempt to discover why so many coats of heraldic arms featured the heads of Africans. The centrepiece of the exhibition was the 60-foot-long *Westminster Tournament Roll* from the College of Arms. At the time, they were researching for an exhibition for Brent Library Service entitled *Roots in Britain: Black and Asian Citizens from Elizabeth I to Elizabeth II*. Audrey 'stopped dead in [her] tracks [and] could hardly believe my eyes' when she saw that one of the six King's trumpeters depicted on the Tournament Roll was a Black African.

As this was before digital reproductions could be exchanged by email or social media, they had to correspond by mail with the College of Arms to ask and pay for the rights to use the image. Their exhibition, *Roots in Britain,* travelled the country for several years. In 1984, Peter Fryer wrote about John Blanke in his seminal book, *Staying Power: The History of Black People in Britain*, having first seen the John Blanke image in 1981 at the touring version of Roots in Britain. He acknowledged in his preface to Staying Power, he 'learnt much' from their exhibition.

As mentioned earlier, it was Dr Sydney Anglo who first recognised 'the blacke trumpet' in the archives. John Blanke goes on to appear in several other entries, as he is paid wages and takes part in the funeral on 11th May 1509 of Henry VII and the following month, 24 June, the coronation of King Henry VIII and Queen Katherine. He also successfully petitions the King for his wages to be doubled. He appears in the 1511 *Westminster Tournament Roll*, leading the opening and closing of the jousting tournament which took place in February that year, which was called to celebrate the birth of Henry VIII's son on New Year's Day that year. His final mention in the records is in January 1512, in which Henry VIII gives instruction for him to be given a gown of violet cloth, and also a bonnet and a hat as wedding presents. The January 1514 listing of the court trumpeters makes no mention of John Blanke, so we can only assume he must have left the court before that date. His entry in Oxford has his dates noted as *John Blanke (fl. 1505-1512)* where fl. stands for *floruit* (Latin for 'he/she flourished'), denoting a date or period during which a person was known to have been alive or active. So, we have some evidence from the court accounts of where and when he was active, as well as some indication of what he looked like from the Tournament Roll.

Those brief accounting entries and his two images, which are little more than caricatures, all raise more questions than answers. Some possible answers were to come from the imaginations of the contributors to the John Blanke Project.

The Project Overview

That original idea of an exhibition developed into *John Blanke Live!*, a series of individual events – an exhibition, symposia and workshops based on the contributions to the project. The activity was supported by the JohnBlanke.com website and its social media presence.

The project's contributions are split into two groups: historians and artists. The commissioning statement for the artists called for an A4 black and white, portrait-format drawing, following on from Stephen's initial contribution. Over time, however, the concept was expanded to offer commissions to photographers, rappers, musicians, playwrights and poets. (None of the artists' works are online, with the exception of the project's founding contribution, Stephen B. Whatley's Tribute to John Blanke, Figure 1.) In addition to their commissioned piece, artists were asked to make a statement beginning 'I imagined John Blanke as…' That statement, along with an image of the artist, is put on the Project's website.

The historians were commissioned to write a thought piece of up to 300 words on some aspect, consequence or interpretation of John Blanke's life or presence that interests or intrigues them. Their complete contribution is made available on the website. The historians include academic, community and independent historians as well as writers, curators, teachers and tour guides.

Artists' Contributions

The project's artists imagined John Blanke in a variety of ways. Many saw him as a musician who is part of the contemporary jazz musician's traditions and heritage; Phoebe Boswell imagined him as the British jazz saxophonist Shabaka Hutchings. Keith Piper saw him as an 'advance guard' for the jazz trumpeter Miles Davis. Some artists envisaged him as a fellow member of the African diaspora, a relative from another time and place. The poet Roy Merchant imagined him as one of his ancestors, while the visual artist Ebun Culwin wrote about him as a fellow member of the diaspora and parent. Others, such as vocal performer Randolph Matthews and visual artist Kimathi Donkor, imagined him as a talented, gifted musician with the will and the confidence to succeed to become chosen by the King to play for him, while others such as Seema Manchanda concluded that, as one of the few Black folk at the Tudor court, he would have been lonely from time to time.

The poet John Agard imagines Blanke blowing 'not quite a fanfare for diversity, simply doing [his] bit for pomp and pageantry'. The late creative director and designer Jon Daniel imagined John Blanke as 'trump card' in a deck of cards, in which Henry VIII was the king, while the poet Mark Thompson sees the rediscovered musician as a 'graphic crowbar' to prise open the cultural door to a better understanding of Black British history.

Each artist reimagined John Blanke in their own, often idiosyncratic, manner. The complete statements of all the artists are reproduced in *Who Is John Blanke?* alongside their individual creative interpretations of John Blanke's image, collectively demonstrating the ingenuity and invention within the artistic imagination.

Historians' Contributions

One of the first historians to make a contribution to the project was Dr Anglo, who modestly stated he could not 'claim a great deal of perspicacity' when he first made the connection between the National Archives and College of Arms archives during his postdoctoral research. I went on to commission other historians, encouraging them to see their contribution as acting as another – more detailed – layer to the responses of the artists. Their contribution was to be related to any part of John Blanke's history or elements of the project that captured their imagination as a historian, based on some aspect of their knowledge, experience and expectations. Many of the historians focused on how tantalising a brief historical record can be. Dr Miranda Kaufmann was frustrated by this imperfect record, which raised more questions than answers. Similarly, Dr Temi Odumosu questioned how we can honour an entire life when there is so much we don't know. Professor Hakim Adi saw that questioning was not a bad thing, but rather a chance to look for evidence that might challenge accepted wisdom. To that end, he saw John Blanke as an 'agent of change'.

The curator Jill Marsh pointed out how portraiture was new at the time and only for high-status individuals. For the common man to have a recognisable portrait was truly exceptional. Dr Onykea cautioned celebrating John Blanke's stardom, as making the trumpeter exceptional made his existence strange and marginalised him. This exceptionalism helps to maintain our prejudices.

The writer and historian Robin Walker questioned the value of that exceptionalism, arguing that for Black Africans to make history, they must shape the world around them in African images and interests. Did John Blanke make those changes? The writer S I Martin considers how John Blanke changes us, seeing him as a mystery – a blank slate on to which we project our duelling notions of Blackness and Britishness.

Change was a theme in several other contributions from historians. For educator Martin Spafford, it was a change in attitudes to race, while teacher Dan Lyndon saw a change in how he taught history. The rapper and historian Phil Day argued Blanke was an example of how migration drives change in history. All the historians' statements are reproduced in full here in *Who Is John Blanke?* The variety of responses from the historians served to demonstrate the impact that John Blanke has on the historical interpretation and imagination, which complemented the contributions of the artists to the project.

John Blanke Live!

The John Blanke Live! Project extended the idea of the exhibition, adding John Blanke symposia and workshops with the strapline 'Art, Archive, Action'. The sheer number of contributions and size of the potential audience meant that initial ideas for a modest exhibition space have been abandoned.

The exhibition is now envisaged as an installation based on Modern Art Oxford 2009 *Polaroids: Mapplethorpe*, in which all the works were black and white and the same size, hung in one continuous line around the gallery space at eye level. All the Project's visual works are black and white, A4 size drawings or photographs, while the poems will be printed on A4 and framed like the visual works, all in the same colour and size black, A3 frames.

Together, the poems and drawings will be hung linearly like Mapplethorpe's *Polaroids*. The 1,828 cm long/37.5 cm wide Great Tournament Roll of Westminster – original or copy – will be fully rolled out and will hang above the drawings, creating a dramatic contrast between its vivid colours and the black and white of the drawings and poems. That dynamic contrast has been exploited in the book design of *Who Is John Blanke?* with all the artists work in black and white and in colour on the cover and in the Great Tournament Roll of Westminster (page 18) and the endpages.

Workshops

The workshops consist of two parts: the first a presentation on who John Blanke was and what he did, ending with an introduction to the project; the second part an invitation for the audience to imagine their John Blanke in an A4 pencil or charcoal drawing workshop. To date, there have been workshops for secondary and primary school pupils, for senior citizens and in a prison. The workshops have subsequently been developed to include one of the artists from the project delivering a drawing class to assist the participants create their interpretation of John Blanke.

Symposia

John Blanke Live! Symposia are open mic sessions, where approximately 15 of the John Blanke Project contributors (a mix of historians, musicians, photographers, writers, poets, artists and rappers) share their interpretation of John Blanke. The artists develop and expand upon their 'I imagined John Blanke as…' statements, while the historians present their view of John Blanke. To date there have been three symposia: at the British Library, College of Arms, and the National Trust Property, Sutton House. The latter two symposia were opened and closed by trumpet fanfares from Corporal Lawrence Narhkom, a Black trumpeter in the British Army currently in the Band of the Grenadiers, whose presence reflects the continuity of the tradition of the Black trumpeter over 500 years in the British army. Each of the symposia has sold out and attracted much praise. More are planned for the future.

Imagination and The John Blanke Project

The strapline for the project is Imagine the Black Tudor trumpeter: imagination is a concept central to the John Blanke Project. The philosopher and educationalist Maratha Nussbaum, in her book *Not For Profit – Why Democracy Needs The Humanities*, argues that the study of Humanities requires a fusion of 'searching critical thought, daring imagination, empathetic understanding of human experiences of many different kinds, and understanding of the complexity of the world we live in' . Nussbaum's view can be developed into a representative model for the production of humanities creative outcomes such as films, books, plays or works of art and the like centered on imagination and critical thinking. Those outcomes are not produced in isolation. Their source is a thought process which begins with intellectual curiosit and imaginative questioning based on a world view.

For the John Blanke Project, for example, those questions were asked at the beginning: Was that his real name? Where did he come from? Whom did he marry? Where did he go after leaving Henry's court? Such questions come from our knowledge of humanities: history, language, culture, religion and consideration of the sheer complexity of the world, rather than taking a constrained parochial or nationalist view. It is the view of a citizen of the world.

Once those questions have been raised, they must be interrogated in a feedback loop between critical thinking and the imagination (see figure 2), within which the critical thinking faculties continually challenge the output of the imagination for acceptability or viability – a potent, fruitful interaction. Eventually, an acceptable creative outcome is finally produced. Critical thinking can be considered as the check or balance on the imagination, applying appropriate restraints were considered necessary. Having produced the creative outcome, intellectual curiosity can come back into play and the process continues. The process, from intellectual curiosity to creative outcome, is shown diagrammatically in figure 2.

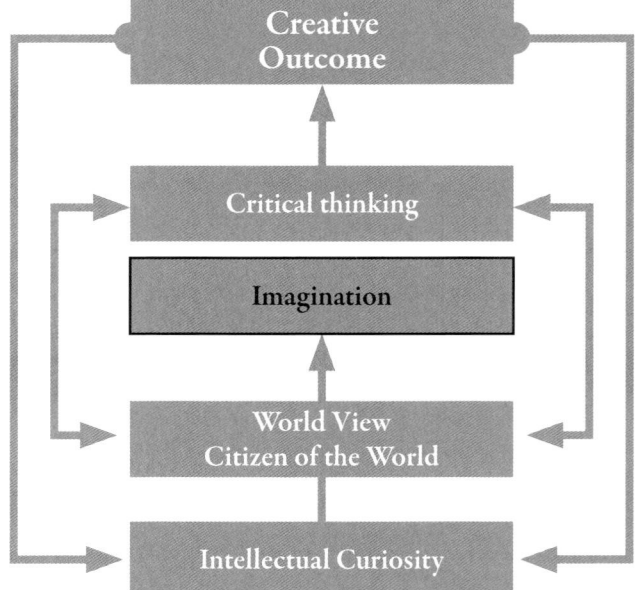

Figure 2. Creative Outcomes

Conclusion

To conclude, through its rich diversity of images and ideas the project has proven to be a novel and inclusive way of telling a piece of Black British history. The contributions have come from artists and historians from a range of ethnicities, genders and ages. Some of the contributors were professional academic, others non-academic or independent, including some based in the community. That rich diversity of minds and bodies is a core strength of the project, enabling it to reach an equally diverse audience.

The publication of the book marks the logical conclusion of my actively commissioning new works for the project. However, from time to time, as and when I encounter an artist or historian with meaningful insights about John Blanke, I will add their contributions to the project online.

The project has demonstrated that when the archival record is exhausted or is brief, we need to look to the imagination take things further, developing the story imaginatively based on the facts, allowing that potent feedback loop (figure 2) between our imagination and critical thinking to take the story on. The creative potential of art, rap, poetry, music and other artistic media to breathe new life into an ephemeral history such as John Blanke's is reflected in the wide range of creative outputs from the project. There are many 'ephemeral histories' in Black British history, such as Pero Jones the enslaved African brought to Bristol in the 18th century to work as domestic servant to a plantation owner, or Sambo an enslaved African boy who died in 1736 at Sunderland Point, Lancashire, and is only remembered through 'Sambo's Grave'. They too have brief, incomplete biographies which, like John Blanke's, have the ability to inspire historians and artists to re-imagine their respective stories and relate them to our contemporary experience, not only telling an authentic and accurate history but completing the circle and making the connections that enable Black British history to become real and relevant for us today.

Michael I. Ohajuru DUniv, FRSA
Senior Fellow Institute of Commonwealth Studies

Notes

Kaufmann, M. (2017, September 01). Blanke, John (fl. 1507–1512), royal trumpeter. Oxford Dictionary of National Biography. Ed. [Accessed online http://www.oxforddnb.com/view/10.1093/ref:odnb/9780198614128.001.0001/odnb-9780198614128-e-107145. 28 Jul. 2018]

Image & Reality: Black Africans in Renaissance England - IRBARE [Accessed online http://irbare2013.weebly.com/ 28 July 2018]

Henry VIII Jousting Before Queen Katharine of Aragon At The Westminster Tournament 1511 (2000) by Stephen B. Whatley, Oil on canvas, 102 x 152cm, Collection of HM Tower of London [Accessed online http://www.stephenbwhatley.com/7_henry-viii-jousting-before-queen-katharine-of-aragon-at-the-westminster-tournament-1511-2000-by-stephen-b-whatley 28 July 2018]

Details of Margureta from Dr Miranda Kaufmann's unpublished doctoral thesis Africans in Britain, 1500-1644. PhD Oxford 2011.

Workshop of Sir Thomas Wriothesley (died 1534), *Westminster Tournament Roll*, painted vellum, 1511 College of Arms, London; repro. in ed. Sydney Anglo, The Great Tournament Roll of Westminster (Oxford: Clarendon Press, 1968), vol. 2, plate 3, membranes 3-5; plate 18, membranes 28-9.

Bindman and Gates, 2010, p52

Kaplan, 1985, p21

Earle and Lowe, 2005, p23

Trexler, 1997, p102

Trexler, 1997, p102

Earle and Lowe, 2005, p 47

Anglo, 1968, p XX

National Archive Exchequer E 36/214, f.109 (The King's Book of Payments: John Blanke's wages, 7 Dec 1507)

Anglo, S., *The court festivals of Henry VII: a study based on the account books of John Heron, Treasurer of the Chamber*, Bulletin of the John Rylands Library. 1960; 43(1): 12-45.

John Blanke Project Historian: Audrey Dewjee [Accessed online http://www.johnblanke.com/audrey-dewjee.html 29 July 2018]

Fryer, 1984, x

John Blanke, Henry VIII's Black Trumpeter, Petitions for a Back Dated Pay [Accessed online Increase https://manyheadedmonster.wordpress.com/2015/07/27/john-blanke-henry-viiis-black-trumpeter-petitions-for-a-back-dated-pay-increase-2/ 30 July 2018]

John Blanke Project Live! [Accessed online http://www.johnblanke.com/jbp-live.html 28 July 2018]

Modern Art Oxford (2009) *Polaroids: Mapplethorpe* [Accessed online https://www.modernartoxford.org.uk/event/exhibition-59/ 28 July 2018]

Nussbaum, (2010), p7

Dresser, M. (2020) Pero's Afterlife: Remembering an Enslaved African in Bristol in Grezina, H. G. (ed) *Britain's Black Past* Liverpool, Liverpool University Press, pp. 119-139

Rice, A. (2020) *Ghostly Presences, Servants and Runaways: Lancaster's Emerging Black Histories and their Memorialization 1687-1865* in Grezina, H. G. (ed) Britain's Black Past Liverpool, Liverpool University Press, pp. 179-195

Bibliography

Ashbee A., *Records of English Court Music, Vol VII 1485-1558* (Snodland, Kent: and Aldershot: Scholar Press) (1986–96)

Anglo, Sydney, ed., *The Great Tournament Roll of Westminster*, Oxford: Clarendon Press (1968) 2 vols

Bindman D. and Gates, Jr H.L. eds., *The Image of the Black in Western Art, Volume II: From the Early Christian Era to the "Age of Discovery", Part 2: Africans in the Christian Ordinance of the World*, Harvard University Press (2010)

Earle, T. F. and Lowe Kate J. P. eds., *Black Africans in Renaissance Europe* (Cambridge: Cambridge University Press (2005).

Fryer, P., Staying Power: *The History of Black People in Britain,* London: Pluto Press (1984)

Kaplan P., *The Rise of the Black Magus in Western Art*, UMI Research Press (1985)

Kaufmann, M. *Black Tudors: The Untold Story*, Oneworld (2017)

Nussbaum M., *Not For Profit – Why Democracy Needs The Humanities*, Princeton University Press (2010)

Olusoga D. *Black and British: A Forgotten History* , Macmillan (2016)

Onyeka, *Blackamoores: Africans in Tudor England, Their Presence, Status and Origins,* Narrative Eye and The Circle with a Dot (2013)

Trexler Richard C., *The Journey of the Magi: Meanings in History of a Christian Story,* Princeton University Press (1997)

The Great Tournament Roll of Westminster

Possibly from the workshop of the Thomas Wriothesley, the Garter King of Arms (1511). The Great Tournament Roll of Westminster, held at College of Arms, London

The painted Roll of the 1511 tournament at Westminster is generally considered to be the greatest treasure possessed by the College of Arms. It was created by artists in the studio of Sir Thomas Wriothesley, Garter King of Arms, probably in the great house which he built in the City of London called Garter House. So far as we know, the Roll has never left the custody of the heralds.

The Roll is made of 36 parchment membranes of various lengths adhered end to end using adhesive. It is nearly 18 metres (59 feet) long and 37 cm wide. The skin membranes vary considerably in thickness and they were fastened together before painting. An extensive range of colours was used in its creation, including gold and silver pigments.

The back of the first membrane of the Roll is covered with a green-coloured textile which served as a cover when the manuscript was rolled. Today the manuscript is in fair condition, although it shows signs of its age with areas of creasing and loss of pigment.

College of Arms

Unrolling the Westminster Tournament Roll.

The Great Tournament Roll of Westminster
Painted on 36 velum membranes
Whole roll 60 feet long and 14 ¾ inches wide

Membranes 3-4
John Blanke seen in the troop of six trumpeters, one of the leading groups in the opening day parade of the tournament 12 February 1511

The sumptuous painting of the Roll commemorates the tournament held by Henry VIII at Westminster on 12 and 13 February 1511, celebrating the birth of a son. Three scenes are depicted. First is the entrance of a procession, including the Knights Challengers. Next comes a view of the tilt, with the participants shown. A dramatic scene has the King on horseback, tilting against an Answerer, watched by the Queen and court from an ornate gallery. Finally, a procession is shown returning from the tournament. These scenes do not present a record of a particular day at the tournament: they are a summary of the festival as a whole and communicate the experiences of those watching. Each procession includes henchmen, heralds, and trumpeters as well as court officials.

The whole Roll, with it concluding verses praising the King, preserves an impressionistic record of the event for future reference. It also presents a narrative sequence in which Henry is set amidst great ceremonies and celebrations: he is put forward as a regal and a chivalric figure. The processions, the heralds and musicians, are all mustered to enhance his power and prestige.

Peter O'Donoghue
York Herald

Membranes 25-26
Henry VIII jousting before Katherine of Aragon and the court, shattering his lance on his opponent's helmet across the barrier

Membranes 27-28
John Blanke seen in the troop of six trumpeters leading the entourage of the victorious Henry VIII and his footmen on the closing day of the tournament 13 February 1511

Artists and Historians

Editor's Note
Miranda Kaufmann and Stephen B. Whatley are listed first among the historians and artists, while all others are arranged alphabetically by surname. They were the very first to be commissioned for this project, and their generosity and remarkable work provided both the inspiration and foundation for the creation of *The John Blanke Project*.

'Although John Blanke is the only Black Tudor we have a picture of, he was by no means the only African in Tudor England'

Dr Miranda Kaufmann
Historian, Writer

John Blanke – A Black Tudor

I've got a photo of John Blanke on my phone, which I show regularly to unsuspecting acquaintances. It may not be the most nuanced portrait of a Black Tudor, but it's the only one I've got. And visually, it does the trick of telling the story that would, as the hackneyed expression goes, take 1,000 words. It's an image that people respond to with surprise and curiosity. They're not used to seeing someone of his complexion in historical dress, let alone on horseback and playing a trumpet decorated with the royal arms.

Seeing John Blanke for the first time conjures up a whole range of questions: the very questions that have formed the basis of my research into Africans in Tudor England. How did he come here? What was his status? Was he enslaved? What was his life like? What happened to him? And, why have I never heard of him before?

Frustratingly, the imperfect record of surviving historical evidence means we can't answer all these questions as completely as I would like. I did my best to lay out all the known evidence of John Blanke's life in the entry I wrote about him in the Oxford Dictionary of National Biography in 2014. Since writing that, I've delved further into the context of Blanke's life, *Black Tudors: The Untold Story* (Oneworld, 2017). Although John Blanke is the only Black Tudor we have a picture of, he was by no means the only African in Tudor England. In my doctoral research into Africans in Britain, 1500-1640, I collected and analysed evidence of over 360 African individuals in early modern parish registers, tax returns, household accounts, court records, letters and diaries. Although many of these records are fragmentary, some fascinating characters emerge: from Jacques Francis, the salvage diver on the Mary Rose, to Christian convert Mary Fillis of Morocco and Reasonable Blackman, the Southwark silk weaver. Africans were living across the country from Hull to Truro, in rural as well as urban locations, and, like John Blanke, they were not enslaved.

I'm really excited about Michael Ohajuru's John Blanke project, because when the archival record is exhausted, we need to let our imaginations take things further. The creative potential of art, poetry and music to breathe new life into history is powerful. I hope that the project goes some way towards the larger goal of putting Black British History in the spotlight. So that seeing an African in historical dress is no longer a surprise. So that film producers no longer believe it would be historically inaccurate to cast a black actor in a Tudor role. And, ultimately, so that we can enjoy a more accurate, full-colour, vision of the British past.

Dr Miranda Kaufmann

For sources see page 259

I imagined John Blanke as both self-assured and soulful. Creating a tribute drawing to John Blanke was both a revelation and revisitation. I had included an interpretation of the black trumpeter in one of my paintings for the Tower of London – of the Westminster Tournament – in 2000; without knowing his identity – but noticing him.

Commissioned to focus on him 15 years later, following a great lecture on black Tudor history by Michael Ohajuru and Dr Miranda Kaufmann, through which I learnt his name and led me to look closer at the original manuscript image

Stephen B. Whatley
Artist

Stephen B. Whatley (2015) *Tribute to John Blanke*, 210 × 297 mm, charcoal on paper

I imagined John Blanke as a seasoned traveller, caught between an unknown world and the only thing known to them. I introduced Cloudface in this image as I felt that they best described the feeling of the distant traveller, the Alien.

Larry Achiampong
Artist

Larry Achiampong (2018) *There Was This Cloud*, photograph

'John Blanke speaks to us in a way that he could never have imagined. His life may not have been too dissimilar to the hundreds of other Africans who were residents in London and other parts of England and Scotland in Tudor times'

Professor Hakim Adi
Professor of the History of Africa and the African Diaspora

John Blanke: An Agent of Change

The image and life history of John Blanke ushers into the dawn of the modern world and perhaps makes us question everything we think we know about it. John Blanke was undoubtedly not the first African to be employed at a royal court in England and certainly not the only one in the early 16th century. He was, like many who would follow him, a musician in the employ of the monarch but that is not his chief significance. That significance lies in the fact that his image has been captured for us in the archival records, as have some other important aspects of his life.

John Blanke speaks to us in a way that he could never have imagined. His life may not have been too dissimilar to the hundreds of other Africans who were residents in London and other parts of England and Scotland in Tudor times. He was a free man and wage earner, a status that was not as common then as it is today. Many of us have been led to believe that in this period Africans could only be free in Africa and wherever else they might appear enslaved status must be assumed. John Blanke and many other Africans in Tudor England demonstrate how inaccurate this assumption has been. He therefore does us a great service, since we can conclude that if there has been one false assumption there might also be many others.

From his petition to the king we know something of the hardship that John Blanke and others faced in this period and that he successfully petitioned for a doubling of his wages, something that few of us would consider today and even fewer would be likely to achieve. John Blanke is therefore one of the first workers on record to successfully demand higher wages and the first African to do so. The fact that he achieved this victory tells us not only something about his skill as a musician but also his status at the Tudor court. Further evidence of this status is shown by his marriage and the wedding present he was given by Henry VIII.

There is no doubt that the few glimpses we have of John Blanke produce as many questions as answers but that is not a bad thing. History is the subject above all others that encourage us to be critical of accepted wisdom and to find the evidence to challenge it. The study of history is after all the study of change and the role that humans play as agents of that change. John Blanke, trumpeter, wage earner and petitioner, was one of those agents but then so are we.

Professor Hakim Adi

I imagined John Blanke as a confident, assured Black man.

A man who knew his own value … his own worth. Indeed so did the King of England, who awarded him not only a pay rise but also special robes to mark royal occasions.

To petition Henry VIII for increased wages illustrates that John Blanke no doubt had the 'gift of the gab'. He was able to put his case in a concise way to obtain a positive outcome.

I imagine him telling stories through his music and voice – a true inspiration to us all.

Sandra A. Agard Hons FRSL
Author, Storyteller and Literature Consultant

A Royal Trumpeter's Tale
By Sandra A. Agard

Let me tell you a story … Are you sitting comfortably? Then I will begin …

Let the trumpets sound …

Here comes the procession of King Henry VII.

This is a special day.

There is going to be a jousting tournament to celebrate the birth of the King's son to his Queen, Katherine of Aragon.

There is great excitement.

The crowds cheer.

The trumpeters hail the entrance of the King.

Their royal livery of gold, red and blues glistening in the morning sunlight.

All the King's horses and all the King's men are here … including someone very special.

Look closely, for you will see him – there … look … look …

A man of the sun.

Everyone is talking about him…for…

He is John Blanke from across the seas.

Some say he came to England's shores with the Spanish Queen Katherine of Aragon as part of her royal court.

Some say he is a Moor and he wears that green headdress with such pride and grace.

John Blanke is a royal trumpeter in the court of Henry VII.

Now, here he is in the procession for King Henry VIII.

Some of the crowd remembered him as he played at the funeral of King Henry VII.

He is indeed a favourite of the court.

He even played at the coronation of Henry VIII.

There is talk that he when Dominic Justinian one of the senior trumpeters died John Blanke actually petitioned the king for Dominic's job and indeed more money – 16d a day no less!

This is not the English way but the king enjoyed John's playing and he got his wage increase – would you believe it? Everybody was talking about how bold John was for days!

The King also gave John Blanke cloths for different tournaments. Yes, he was such a favourite of Henry VIII.

However, what is the end of this royal trumpeter's tale known as John Blanke?

Haa … that is another story to be told another day.

The End?

© Sandra A. Agard 2020

I Imagined John Blanke as not backward in coming forward, daring to write to the King requesting a rise in pay, I imagine John Blanke to be a man aware of his own contribution to the royal retinue of trumpeters.

I imagine John Blanke as a dignified presence yet possessing a wry sense of humour. I can see him playing a game of chess with a Tudor mate, and suddenly breaking into classical Arabic كش ملك 'Kish Malek' (Checkmate!) just to test the puzzled expression on the white faces surrounding him.

I also imagine him as a man with consideration for his neighbours. I don't imagine him practising syncopated riffs on his trumpet just after midnight. That wouldn't go down too well with a leafy suburban Tudor postcode!

John Agard
Poet and Playwright

John Blanke
By John Agard

In Norman French the name has a ring that's nice
Not John Blanke, John Blanc, to be precise

Shall we say a Tudor gentleman of colour?
Or one who brought colour to the Tudor court?
What's in a name leaves ample room to ponder
for am I not John White the Black
and Black John White rolled into one turban?

In days when the Henrys ruled the royal roost
And the King himself took to the manly joust
I hailed the thrust of lance with trumpet blast.
I, the equestrian exotic of the retinue,
Blowing for every pence of my shillings' due

Thus the North African winds had followed me
to an England known both as Olde and Merry.
Yes, I whose Moorish skin echoed midnight's key,
surveyed from a turban's rainbow my adopted Albion.
And to those white cliffs my lips put forth their clarion.

Not quite a fanfare for diversity.
Simply doing my bit for pomp and pageantry.
Yet when history's footnotes begin to grow more bold
and the heart's tapestry unrolls its spectrum,
hear again my trumpet's dark riffs rising out of vellum.

© John Agard 2016

'[T]his confirmation of [John Blanke's] existence and political agency corrects and projects a more complete history of African people in the UK's past, into the future'

Dr Toyin Agbetu
Community Educator

John Blanke: Exposes the Simplistic 'Black' Presence Narrative in British History as an Afriphobic Fabrication

I am a scholar-activist.

My journey to recognise that identity has been a long one. Realising my compulsion to change our world for the better by synthesising the world of my imagination with that shaped by 'knowledge' has been challenging. But the seed of my passion starts with my childhood. Back then I loved watching science fiction. However there was a huge gap in the genre, African people did not exist, at least in central characters. At the most we were depicted as 'blacked' Europeans in peripheral roles. It was a void not truly filled in me until as an adult I started on a journey reading authors like Octavia Butler, Walter Mosley, Nalo Hopkinson and later Courttia Newland and Nnedi Okorafor. Suddenly this anomaly was repaired as I realised, to paraphrase Einstein – the power a holistic fusion of imagination and intellect can bring to rigorous scholar-activism.

But I suspect that the young Toyin explored the future because here in the UK he was taught a version of British history where there were no Africans, at least not unless they were enslaved. The evidenced revelation of John Blanke's existence as a trumpeter in the early 16th century helps destroy this myth.

Far from being an early example of the misused term 'political correctness', his visual presence in the Art of the 1511 Westminster Tournament Roll and his references in the Treasury Archives is the result of scholarly research. It exposes the fact that the simplistic rendition of the African presence in colonial British history to a myopic 'slavery to Empire Windrush' narrative is an Afriphobic fabrication, a revisionist attempt to deny the presence of self-determining Africans in the UK predating Maafa.

It would be good to have details of Blanke's personal story, but thankfully this confirmation of his existence and political agency corrects and projects a more complete history of African people in the UK's past, into the future. It is now for us to continue imagining and intellectually excavating details of other Africans whitewashed from British history.

Dr Toyin Agbetu

For sources see page 259

I Imagined John Blanke as an enchanting figure who transcends history and the boundaries of reality and legend, situated at the nexus where myth and historical fact converge. In reimagining him, I saw not merely a musician in a royal procession but a mythical embodiment of Tudor England's grandeur. His presence – stalwart, dignified, and captivating – defined the aura of every parade and tournament, particularly the jousts, symbolising something far greater than the moment itself.

This act of reimagining speaks to the theoretical concept of mythopoeia, the creation of myth where the evidence of history is immaterial (Tolkien, 1965). Drawing from thinkers like Barthes, who posited that myth is a system of communication through which cultural narratives are constructed and sustained (Barthes, 1972, p. 107), I have embraced artistic liberty to conceive a heroic legend. This legend, like that of King Arthur or the deities of ancient Greece, emerges from the lacunae of recorded history, filling these voids with imagination, wonder, and speculative futures.

In this space where history recedes, myth rises to forge an identity not solely tethered to the past but forward-looking. The process of mythmaking becomes a means of cultural survival and evolution (Campbell, 1949). As understood through Jungian archetypes, myths tap into the collective unconscious, offering a shared narrative framework (Jung, 1964). Though veiled by time, figures such as John Blanke become touchstones for a broader reflection on Black identity, history, and the future, especially when considered through the lens of Afrofuturism (Eshun, 2003).

In this spirit, I conceived John Blanke as not merely a historical figure but as the 'Sarkin Kakakin Sarauta' (Hausa: King of the Royal horn blowers), a being imbued with the strength, grace, and nobility often reserved for mythic heroes. Here, I invoke the centaur, an archetype embodying the balance between instinct and intellect, tradition and transformation, familiar in the works of Campbell on the hero's journey. Yet, unlike the centaur's archer, whose bow and arrow represent focus and attack, my John Blanke wields a kakaki horn – a symbol of resonance, power, and voice. The kakaki here does more than signify his historical role; it becomes a metaphor for amplifying marginalised voices, a tool of liberation, calling forth new futures where Black existence is no longer peripheral but central to the narrative.

This kakaki becomes a symbol in line with Afrofuturist theory, which reclaims Black history by projecting it into the future, as scholars like Eshun and Dery have suggested (Dery, 1994). Afrofuturism reconfigures myth and fantasy as vehicles for cultural reclamation, engaging the African diaspora in reimagining its past and future, free from the confines of colonial narratives. Through this lens, John Blanke is not simply a figure resurrected from history; he becomes an Afrofuturist icon, merging the ancestral with the speculative, the historical with the mythical. Like the sonic technologies of Afrofuturist imagination, his kakaki is a call to both remembrance and revolution.

In this artistic reimagining, John Blanke is not merely a passive relic of the past but a dynamic mythical figure whose legacy pulses with the energy of cultural resistance, resilience, and future possibility. Though obscured by the annals of time, his story now resonates as a symbol of heroism, wisdom, and the enduring human spirit, projected into a future where Blackness reclaims its place at the centre of history, myth, and cosmic possibility.

Barthes, R. (1972). *Mythologies*. New York: Hill and Wang.
Campbell, J. (1949). *The Hero with a Thousand Faces*. Princeton: Princeton University Press.
Dery, M. (1994). *Flame Wars: The Discourse of Cyberculture*. Durham: Duke University Press.
Eshun, K. (2003). *More Brilliant than the Sun: Adventures in Sonic Fiction*. London: Quartet Books.
Jung, C. G. (1964). *Man and His Symbols*. London: Aldus Books.
Tolkien, J. R. R. (1965). *The Monster and the Critics and Other Essays*. London: HarperCollins.

Hassan Aliyu FRSA, (DProf, Fine Art – UEL)
Artist/Curator

Hassan Aliyu (2020) *John Blanke*, 210 × 290 mm, ink on paper

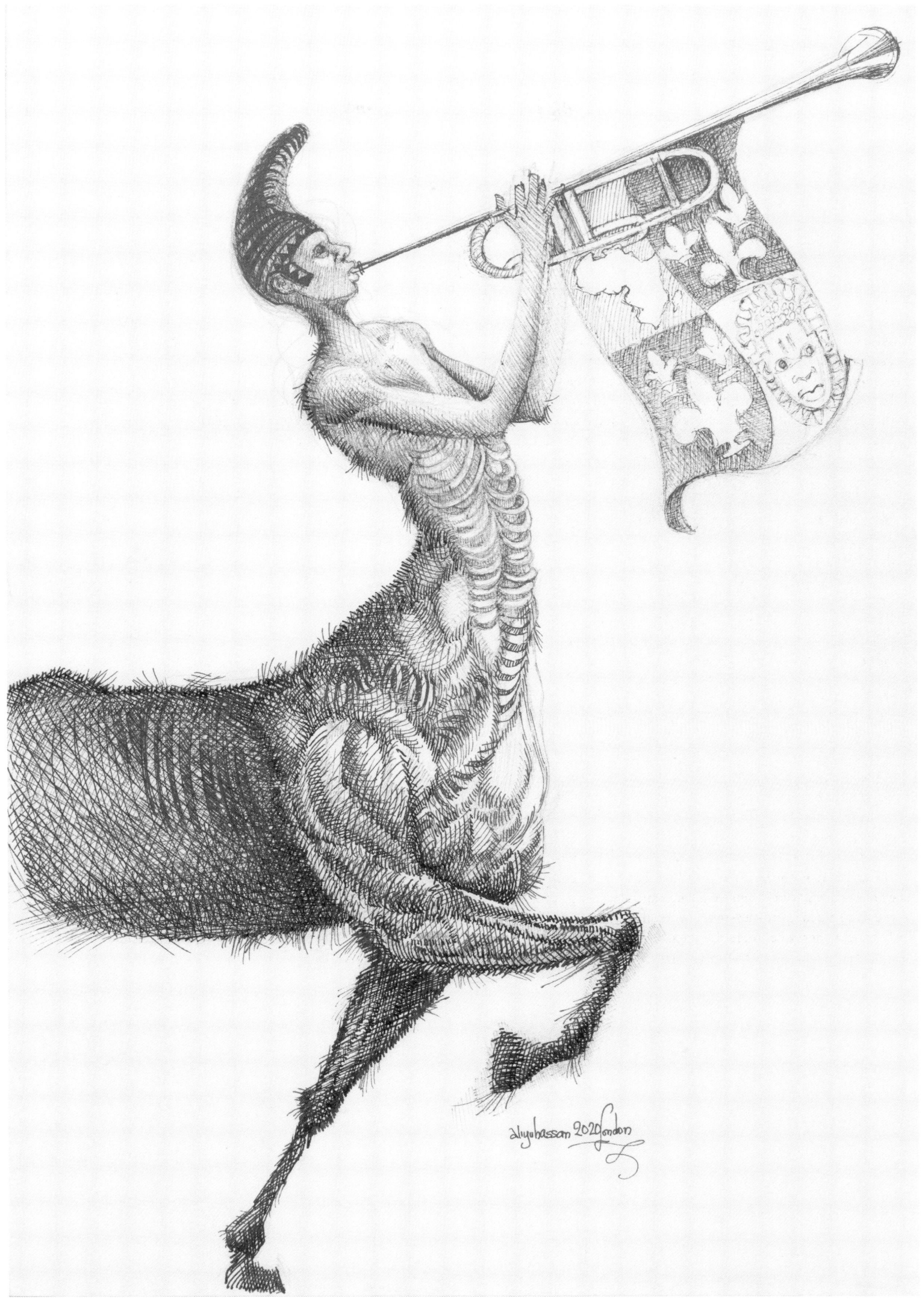

'The only black trumpeter mentioned [paid by Henry VIII's chancellor] must be the only black trumpeter depicted in the Great Tournament Roll'

Dr Sydney Anglo
Private correspondence Dec 2012
Used with permission

The Historian Who First Identified John Blanke

Dr Sydney Anglo was the first to recognise the connection between the John Blanke depicted in the Art of the 1511 Westminster Tournament Roll and his references in the Archives in the accounts of John Heron Treasurer to Henry VII and Henry VIII.

John Blanke was brought to our attention as a footnote by Dr Sydney Anglo in the Bulletin of John Rylands Library xliii Volume 43 1960-1961 in an article entitled 'The Court Festivals of Henry VII: a study based on the account books of John Heron, Treasurer of the Chamber' by Sydney Anglo, B.A., Ph.D., Research Fellow of the University of Reading. The footnote read:

> *3 I believe this John Blank [sic] was, in fact, a Negro in the Great Roll of the Tournament at Westminster in February 1511, preserved at the College of Arms, a negro musician is twice depicted amongst the king's trumpets. This I think was John Blank, the "blacke trumpet".*
>
> Anglo, S., *The court festivals of Henry VII: a study based on the account books of John Heron, Treasurer of the Chamber,* Bulletin of the John Rylands Library. 1960; 43(1):12-45.

Here Dr Anglo describes how he made the discovery:

> *My discovery that John Blanke, the 'Blacke Trompette' in [John] Heron's Accounts was, in fact, depicted in the Great Tournament Roll of Westminster was purely the result of straightforward historical research in the very distant past (the mid 1950s) when I was a postgraduate student preparing for a Ph.D thesis on Early Tudor Court Festivals under the supervision of Frances Yates at the Warburg Institute.*
>
> *I was working my way systematically through the Account Books of John Heron Treasurer of the Chamber (preserved at the public Record Office), covering the reigns of Henry VII and Henry VIII and there under December 7th 1507 was the first of several payments of wages to 'John Blanke 'the blacke trumpet'.*
>
> *At about the same time I was also working on manuscripts at the College of Arms among which, of course, was the Great Tournament Roll of Westminster. There I found two representations of 'Les Trompettes' the first at membranes 3-4 which included a black trumpeter in the middle of the second row of three; and the second at membranes 27-28, 'Le son des Trompettes. A lostel' with the black trumpeter again in the second row.*
>
> *I fear I cannot claim a great deal of perspicacity in recognising that the only black trumpeter mentioned by Heron must be the only black trumpeter depicted in the Great Tournament Roll. On the other hand I must admit that I still take pleasure in the identification and in the fact that the heraldic artist responsible was meticulous enough to record John Blanke's presence.*

Dr Sydney Anglo

John Blanke entry in 1507 Court Accounts
National Archive NA: PRO, E 36/214 109

I imagined John Blanke as a commanding figure, vibrant and full of life, his presence a harmonious blend of dignity and artistry. As I prepare to paint, I see him standing tall, the sunlight glinting off his gilded trumpet, poised in mid-performance at the heart of Henry VIII's court. His gaze is steady and confident, a subtle defiance against the norms of the time. I imagine rich fabrics in deep, bold hues framing his figure, the textures a nod to his African heritage and Tudor England's opulence. Around him, the court is a swirl of motion and sound, yet he remains the centerpiece – a symbol of resilience and cultural intersection, embodying a story far larger than himself.

Text
Artificial intelligence – ChatGPT BlackBritHist

Image
Artificial intelligence – Midjourney

Artificial Intelligence – Midjourney (2023)

I imagined John Blanke as an individual who took pride in his musical role despite the difficulties he most likely encountered, given the period in history and the nature of his role as trumpeter for the King. Having so much mystery and ambiguity around him, I imagined him turning towards his passion for music to find meaning and motivation, all the while having the unique experience of being black in this role at this time.

Year 9 Student at Kings Priory School, North Shields

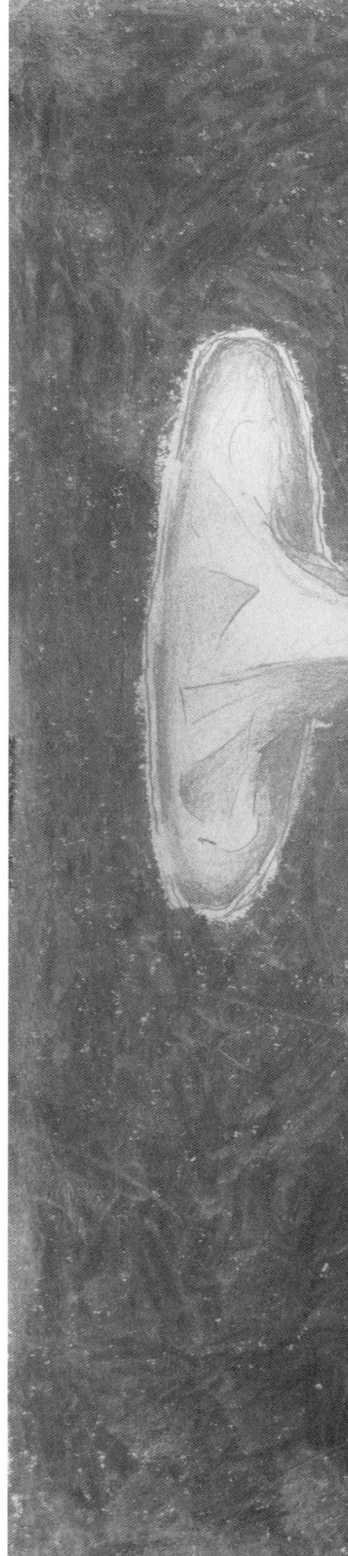

Year 9 Student (2023) *John Blanke*, 418 × 297 mm, mixed media

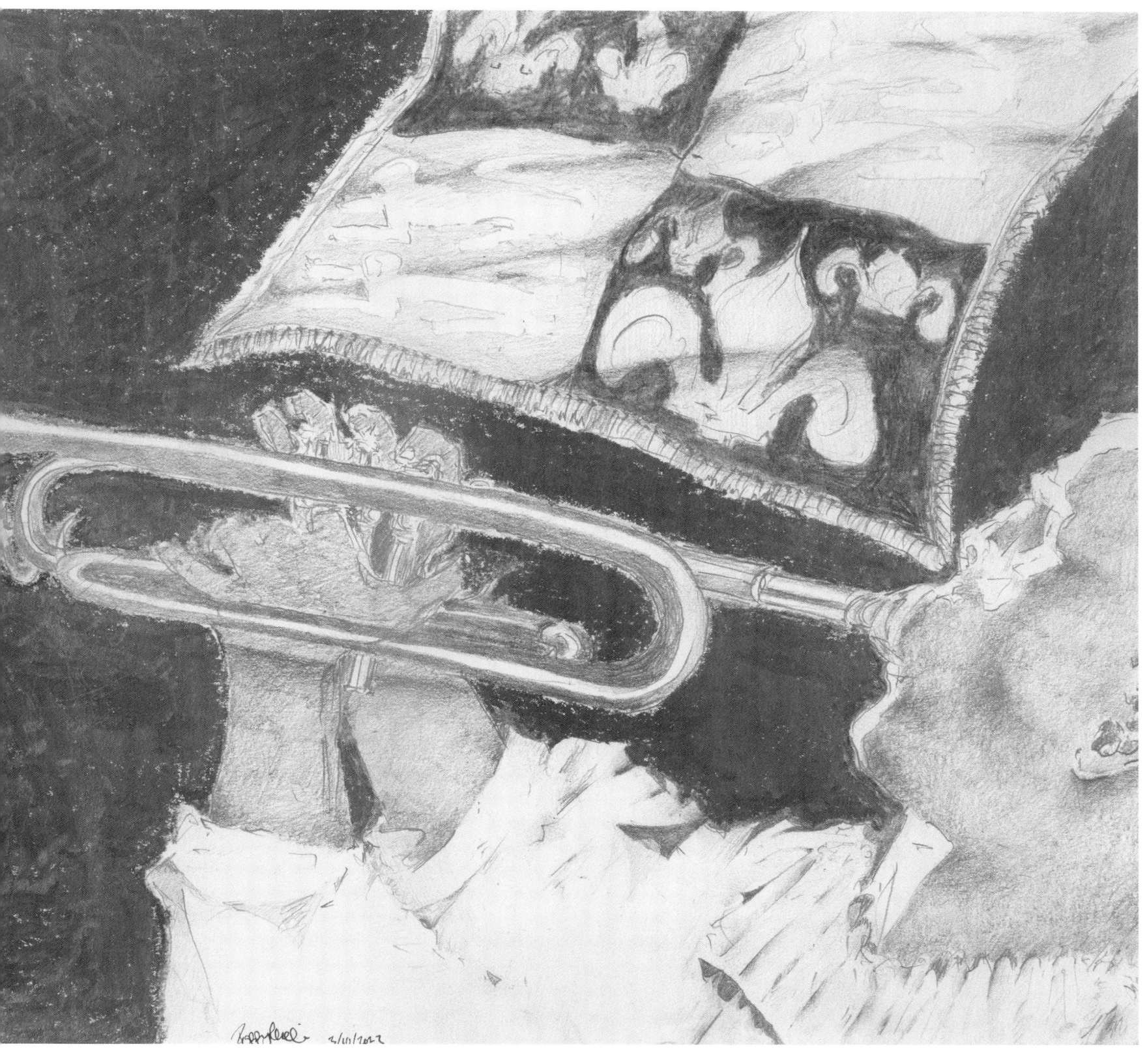

I imagined John Blanke as an international sound pioneer and global trader of groundbreaking audio niceness. He has achieved what all migrants achieve, breaking out from national borders to test the world's ability to accept change and innovation. Whether by choice or enforced, John Blanke – who changed his name from 'Blacke' to help smooth his path in a world that struggles to accept the direct power of Blackness – is a person who uses the tools at his disposal to travel widely and express himself freely.

Toby Laurent Belson
Artist

Toby Laurent Belson (2018) *John Blanke*, digital print

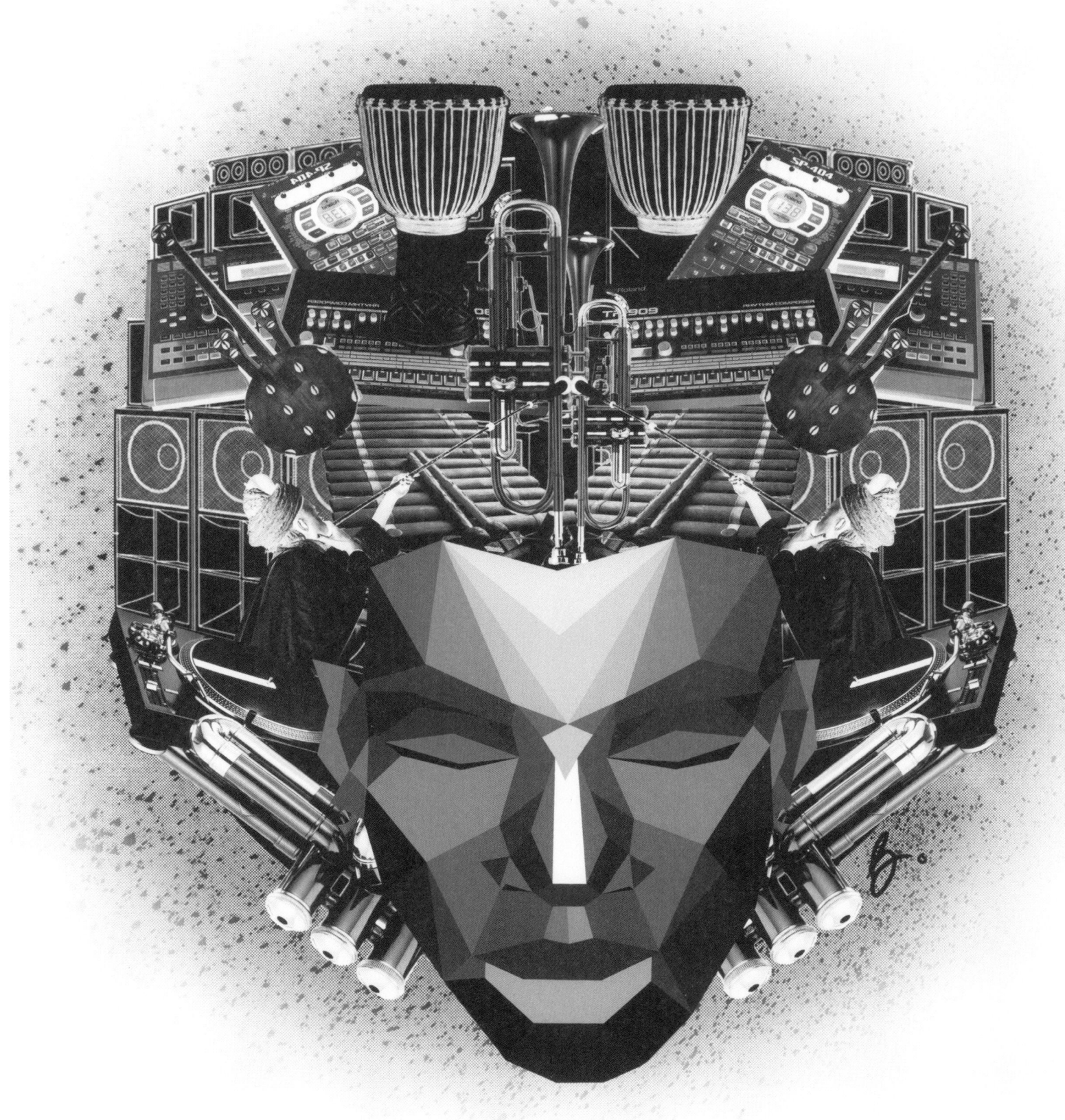

'The most unusual thing about John Blanke is not that he was a musician or that he was at the English court or that he was thought well of, but that he was pictured at all'

David Bindman
Emeritus Professor of the History of Art

John Blanke the black trumpet

There is much that is remarkable about the image in the sixty-foot long Westminster Tournament Roll of 1511 in the College of Arms, of a black trumpeter on horseback. The most striking is that we know his name, John Blanke, and there are payments recorded to him over a decade, and he seems to have been shown particular favour by King Henry VIII. These payments make it clear that he was not a slave but a salaried member of the court. In any case he lived before Britain's entry into the slave trade initiated in 1562-63 by Sir John Hawkins.

So where did John Blanke come from and how did he get to England? The short answer is that we do not know, but it is likely that as a skilled musician he would have made his way through court circles which were always interacting with each other. It is possible he started his career in Spain, to which he could have crossed from Africa, and through more northern courts. The other possibility is that he could have come directly from Spain in the retinue of Catherine of Aragon, who is known to have had at least some black women with her when she first arrived in 1501. There were also black mentioned at the Scottish court at the time so that is another possibility.

In a way the most unusual thing about John Blanke is not that he was a musician or that he was at the English court or that he was thought well of, but that he was pictured at all. He was not the first black person to be depicted in English art; there are images of the black Magus in the Adoration of the Magi in stained glass and manuscript illuminations of the 15th century but nothing else is known from the first half of the 16th century. But the fact that John Blanke was a real person with a profession and a name makes the image of him a priceless survival and a national document of the highest importance.

David Bindman

I imagine John Blanke as an intelligent, ambitious soul with an adventurous, brave spirit. He knows his worth and has no reason to doubt it. He is accepted for who he is and for the accomplished musician he has become. He is a man who can say, I see, and I AM SEEN, in the brightness of day, not consigned to shadows.

Hazel Blue
Artist

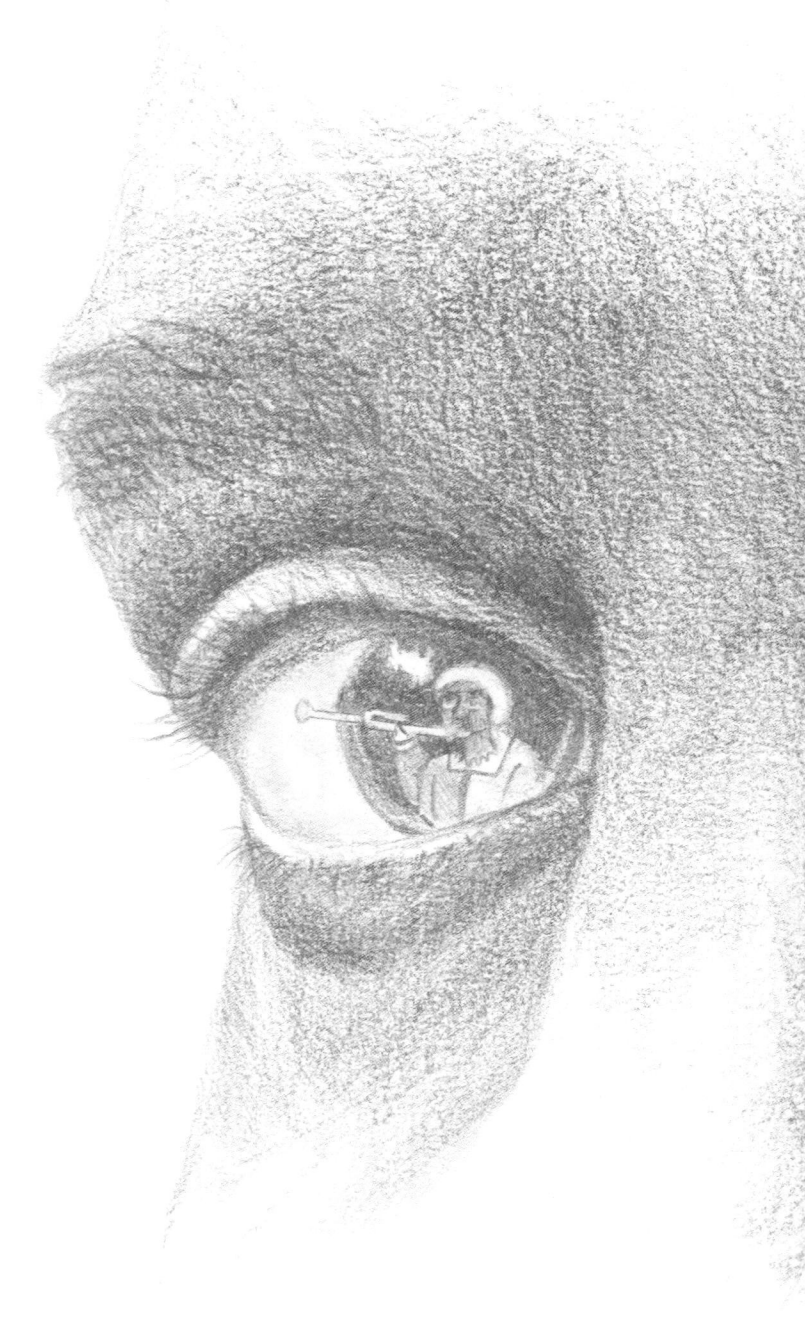

Hazel Blue (2024) *John Blanke*,
210 × 297 mm, pencil on card

I imagined John Blanke as Shabaka Hutchings. I like serendipitous things. On the same day that I was introduced to the idea – the memory – of John Blanke and asked to consider his portrait, the importance of his presence in history, and my interpretation of it, I also had the pleasure of seeing the extraordinary saxophonist Shabaka Hutchings perform and speak about his idea of belonging – of the space between – as a child of the diaspora, a Londoner, a musician, classically trained and trained by life, by heart, and by geography. I knew that it would be in drawing Shabaka that I'd find my John Blanke. Because when I hear Shabaka play, I can hear that I exist, and when we see that John Blanke existed, we know we can play.

Phoebe Boswell
Artist

Phoebe Boswell (2015) *Shabaka Hutchings as John Blank*e, 330 × 227 mm, pencil on paper

'John Blanke has always been in my mind. He is one of many early "signposts" to Britain's post-war, post-Windrush black community'

Stephen Bourne
Writer and Historian

A Massive Jigsaw Puzzle

In the 1970s I was still at school when I began to look for history books about black people in Britain. In those days they were rare but not impossible to find. Inter-library loans and the multicultural bookshop near my home on Peckham High Street were a great help.

My early discoveries included Edward Scobie's *Black Britannia* (1972) and Folarin Shyllon's *Black People in Britain 1555-1833* (1977). From reading these books I realised that they were the tip of a huge iceberg, a massive jigsaw with many pieces. I felt that it would take more than one lifetime to piece this story together, but I undertook the journey anyway to explore my personal interests in black Britons from history.

John Blanke is mentioned in Peter Fryer's *Staying Power* (1984), but I cannot say for certain if this was my introduction to Henry VIII's black musician. John Blanke has always been in my mind. He is one of many early 'signposts' to Britain's post-war, post-Windrush black community.

The now familiar image of him playing a trumpet on the 1511 Westminster Tournament Scroll was imprinted on my mind years ago, but I cannot remember where I first saw this. Could it have been featured on a postcard? If so it will be buried somewhere in one of my eight filing cabinets, now bursting with information about black Britons, collected over 40 years.

In 2005 I discovered my own 'Black Tudor', John Primero, described as "a negro" in the 1607 baptism record of my local church, St Giles's in Camberwell. He was buried there in 1615. Over time I have kept an open mind about black history because I never know what piece of the jigsaw I am going to read about or discover next.

Stephen Bourne

I imagine John Blanke as a strong-minded individual, but also living in fear, a man who has been taken from his homeland and forced to play the Trumpet for the King of England. A land at that time which had very little respect for black people. Who knows whether it was against his will or not? He may have been in a high position, but was this what he wanted? Was he a free man?

Nathan Bowen
Street Artist

Nathan Brown (2018) *John Blanke*, 210 × 297 mm, felt tip pen on paper

'a constituent part of our common history'

Jeff Bowersox
Associate Professor

John Blanke's Legacy: Unveiling the Long History of the Black Presence in England and Germany

John Blanke's story tells us something profoundly mundane: Black people lived in Britain a very long time ago. This is profound chiefly because of conventional narratives that presume otherwise, but in most ways this is a mundane fact. Some few Black residents, like John Blanke, were fortunate to be successful, close to seats of power and influence, and this is why we can have some insight into his existence. In this way, John Blanke's story connects Britain to the continent, as his counterparts can be found in the German-speaking lands too.

There is a longer history dating back at least to the Black advisors, guards, and servants who populated the Hohenstaufen court in the 12th and 13th centuries. Scholars like Anne Kuhlmann-Smirnov and Rashid-S. Pegah have found and catalogued many Black servants in Renaissance and early modern courts, many of whom occupied musical roles not dissimilar to John Blanke's. Even at a minor court like the one at Bayreuth we can find a timpanist and actor named Christian Ferdinand, who made a good living there from the 1660s and had four children with his wife Susanna Clara. Like John Blanke, he shows up in a couple of illustrations of processions, but he was not alone. He worked with and may well have been trained by another Black timpanist named Eberhard Christoph, who was married to a widow named Maria Jakobina and had one daughter.

We should resist the temptation to romanticise everything about their life courses. Christian Ferdinand, at least, found his way to the courts via networks of enslavement, and others in similar positions protested against what they considered unfair treatment. But we should include what we know of their presence, their roles, their opportunities, and their frustrations as a constituent part of our common history.

Jeff Bowersox

For sources see page 260

I imagined John Blanke as a majestic musician, a professional who knew his worth, and a proud Black man bearing his heritage in his sound and in his soul.

Who was John Blanke? There are records that seem to pin him into position: a man on a horse playing a trumpet at the Westminster Tournament; a petition to King Henry VIII for a wage increase; an inventory of wedding clothes gifted by the King. Yet he remains a puzzle, a conundrum, a perennial question mark.

Who is he to us today? Records are still emerging that may tell us more – and different – stories about this man. Intriguing new discoveries in the archive spark exciting new questions. Perhaps, more than anything, John Blanke teaches us that history is alive, breathing, ever-changing; that the past is still full of possibilities.

Joanna Brown
Writer and Educator

Black Trumpet
By Joanna Brown

I know my worth.
You cannot put a price on genius, but you can give me
    my due.
I played for dark-skinned kings and queens long
    before I played for you.

Africa, where all stories, and my first memories began.
Life; breath; music.
At birth I learned to listen.
My mother, pouring songs sweet as love into my ear.
My father, whispering prayers soft as secrets over
    my head.
Inspiration, exhalation.
Spirit; soul; sound.

As the dawn bright birds shimmered out of the
    forest's emerald cloak
I laughed in careless harmony with my brothers
    and sisters.
At dusk, when the sky drew down her indigo veil
    over the heaving sea,
I sat, cross-legged, and listened to the storied
    wisdoms of my elders.
I have moved with them all in dances deeper
    than time.
We are bound together by our shared sound.
Home is a circle of many.

Later, on a journey charted by stars
I came to know the rise and fall of an endless ocean,
the rhythm of ancient water, the cadence of
    lunar tides.
The silent ache of absence.

Now, into your courts of walled stone and gilded
    tapestry
with curved brass I sound my own majestic history,
blasting my sea-soaked memories
with yearning, with urgency,
into the feast-smoked air.
Look there –
and see my ancestors move through these tall halls
in procession proud as pavane.
Hear me play, and rise like royalty.

Dance, held by spell of notes woven from
    times past and now –
an iridescence of melody.
Step into the realm of a partner's arc, and circling
    the rustle of satin black
lift hands; show palms;
eyes locked
in promise of possibility.

My music marks your exits and your entrances,
    punctuating your passage
in and out of the Great Halls,
in and out of life itself.
My breath heralds the death
of one king; the crowning of another;
the birth of a doomed son.

Westminster. The tournament.
A pageantry of flags, scarlet serpents rippling
    the iron sky.
Out on the field, the stamp and thunder of
    snorting horses,
kicking up clods of blood-thirsty earth.
A warrior king.
The dissonant clash of metal-clad men.

But then – a woman, dark with the beauty of
    ocean midnight,
clothed in gold,
her braided hair adorned with jewels like beaded
    droplets of rain,
plays an akonting,
plucks silver notes like stars from a taut string,
sings in a voice as high and clean and clear as a
    mountain spring.
My heart is caught!

Dress me in violet – the colour of kings.
Palms meet in promise;
an exchange of rings.

Now let my story end as this last dance begins.

© Joanna Brown 2024

I imagined John Blanke as an incredibly talented, dedicated musician, enjoying his elite position as court trumpeter and confidently aware of the value of the gift he shared. I love the horn in contemporary music and was listening to South African jazz while thinking about this commission. So my portrait of John Blanke is inspired by the superbly talented Johannesburg-based trumpeter, composer and bandleader Mandla Mlangeni.

Victoria Burgher
Artist

Victoria Burgher (2018) *John Blanke*, 210 × 297 mm, woodcut

I imagined John Blanke as an exceptional musician/trumpeter ... with a cool commanding energy and dynamic spirit. ... After some research I felt inspired to make a spontaneous aquatint etching which I've embellished with subversive bindis and Swarovski gems to give John Blanke a regal and anarchic quality I think he represents and deserves!

Chila Kumari Burman
Artist

Chila Kumari Burman (2106) *John Blanke*, 290 × 210 mm, carton etching on card with bindi and faux gems

I imagined John Blanke as:

Someone who strived to use his skills to succeed.

Someone whose name and image echo from the past to the present.

Someone who knew his worth and whose actions demonstrate the essence of humanity; that we are each no lesser or greater than one another.

Jody Burton
Artist

Jody Burton (2017) *John Blanke*, 210 × 297 mm, pencil on paper

John Blanke the Blacke trumpeter
Westminster Tournament Roll 1511
In the reign of King Henry VIII

I imagined John Blanke as a reflection of myself. Illustrated that as long as there is life there is hope, for his and future generations, for people of colour. Despite all the obstacle put before him, he realised through the gift of his Art/Music he could invoke emotions and give hope. John Blanke songs of freedom.

Rohan Clarke
Artist

Rohan Clarke (2016), *John Blanke*, 210 × 297 mm

I imagined John Blanke as a small delicate guy living in barracks, and being careful about fitting in, avoiding arguments. He did his musical tasks, and he must have impressed a few important people, because he's in a painting. Was he tripped up and mocked all the time, and was always nervous, or was it nothing like that? Race is a hostile idea, it's a historic weirdness, its purpose is largely economic exploitation. Capitalism began its big present global phase in his lifetime. Where could we go to conquer and colonise, to get their resources and increase our markets? Whose humanity could we crush and rape? Looking at the endlessly dense psychology of perceptions of race, the psychology of Othering, often involves skipping around the basic horrible fact of exploitation. Britain's history in relation to race is about the worst of any nation ever. At the moment racial difference is used as a rabble-rousing concept by right-wing and far-right political leaders. Again Britain is a terrible offender. What could I possibly imagine about this blank Blanke that has a chance of being anything like his reality? There seems to be virtually nothing known about the subject of my picture, beyond extremely basic notions, and a possible – much simplified and stylised – likeness in a historic painting. I like the fact that Blancke or Blak is recorded as having two opposite names – it's obviously a very resonant ambiguity. I also like the solid materialism of the category of the only bit of information about him that's indisputable: his pay. He received eight pence a day, he successfully petitioned the King at one point to double it. There's a record of a payment to him for one month, of 20 shillings. The beautiful Westminster Tournament roll portrait of Blancke/Blak was the visual basis for my painting. I did five versions eventually.

Matthew Collings
Artist

Matthew Collings (2020) *John Blanke*, 210 × 297 mm, mixed media

J. BLANCKE or BLAK

8 pence a day

Brenda

I imagined John Blanke as a fellow diaspora musician and parent. I feel his life as if he is a member of my family. I identify with his courage and strong spirit in requesting the same pay as his fellow white trumpeters. Sometimes even unbeknown to ourselves, our courage for the sake of our family and self-dignity, causes us to make positive action that moves us out of our comfort zone. This kind of action, I believe, can make a difference not just in our lives, but ripple into others' lives, far into the future. I identify with the causes I actively make in my own life.

My triptych reflects this feeling. I wanted to create a timeline from past to present. To further my connection, I made this preliminary study of a contemporary artist and close friend, as the face of John Blanke.

Ebun Culwin
Artist

Ebun Culwin (2019) *Triptych – Future. Present, Past*
3 boards, 300 × 250 mm, pencil on paper, acrylic on board

Ebun Culwin (2019) *John Blanke*
210 × 297 mm, pencil on paper

'Are the 1507 John Blanke (sic) Trumpeter and 1488 John Blank (sic) Footman one and the same person?'

Sean Cunningham
Head of Medieval Records, The National Archives

History is Always Moving Forward

Our knowledge of previous events, people and places is only deepened and refreshed by the work of historians, researchers and interpreters when they add new layers of knowledge to the material of history which we inherit. We should embrace this process. By looking back in more focussed ways at an increasing range of evidence, we get a fuller picture of what happened in the past. What might be key facts would otherwise remain annoyingly out of reach until new work reveals how they fit into the familiar narrative. The past then glides into sharper focus through the drawing forward of small details and isolated fragments from often obscure areas.

This is the case with John Blanke. After he was first identified as the black trumpeter paid wages in 1507, seen in in the Westminster tournament roll picture from 1511 and the records of the cloth given out at the funeral of King Henry VII in 1509, it became easier to look for him elsewhere in the historical record. Knowing his job as a royal musician meant that it should only have been a matter of time until more documents appeared. Some were soon found, including John's petition for increased wages in 1512, Henry VIII's gift of cloth for his wedding around the same time, and his appearance at state events, like the king's coronation in June 1509.

More unexpected was a new reference to John Blank (sic) as a footman in Henry VII's personal service in 1488. An earlier date and a different job calls for some re-evaluation of John's life story. It proves that our understanding can never stand still and that we have to be ready to accept accurate new information when it appears. This is how we achieve a more reliable impression of what the past was truly like for all our ancestors.

Sean Cunningham

For sources see page 259

The National Archive (101/412/20)

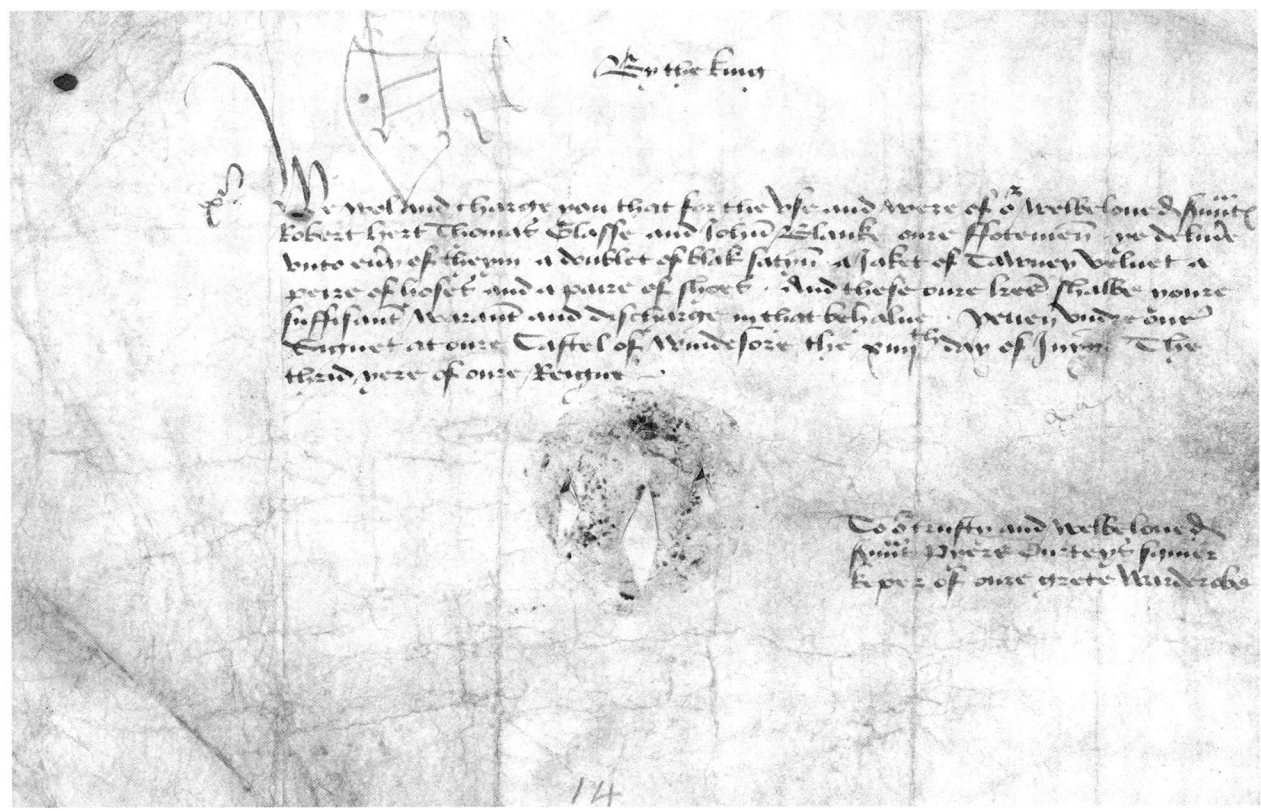

I imagined John Blanke as the firstborn son of Nana Damoah, born at sunrise on a beautiful Saturday in June. Being born on that day, he was given the name Kwame, the Akan tradition for boys born on Saturdays.

Living in the Kingdom of Dagomba, Kwame looked up to his father, a rich merchant and a well-travelled man fluent in multiple African and European languages. Each time before Nana left for Europe, Kwame begged his father to allow him to come along, for he missed his father dearly during the months that he was gone. And when Nana returned, Kwame would sit with him and listen closely as he shared the wonderful stories of his adventures abroad.

One day, Nana returned with a present for Kwame: a trumpet wrapped in a soft red cloth. The minute he laid eyes on the trumpet, Kwame was determined to practise and practise and practise until he mastered the instrument. He was going to make his father proud. So he took his new trumpet to his music teacher and said, 'I need to learn. Will you help me?'

And his music teacher did. By the time he turned nineteen, Kwame knew his way around that trumpet better than he knew his own bedroom at home. He played for his father one night, and when he blew his last note, his father jumped to his feet and embraced him.

'You're ready, my son,' said Nana.

Kwame looked into his father's face – looked at the pride in his father's face – and smiled widely. 'I can come with you to Europe?' he asked, barely containing his excitement.

'Yes,' his father said. 'We leave for England in two days.'

It took them a full year to get to England. They started in the Gulf of Guinea, moving on to Morocco, Spain, Portugal, France, and at last Felixstowe, England. Each place brought new experiences for Kwame, and he loved every minute of it. He loved that he was finally travelling the world with his father, a dream he'd been chasing for as long as he could remember.

Nana had friends in England, so Kwame and his father stayed with them in a lovely small town called Welling in the county of Kent. Nana's friends, John and Pat, were also merchants. When he learned that fact, Kwame could not stop asking them questions about their travels. He developed a particularly strong friendship with John, who liked telling stories just as much as Kwame liked hearing them. But John had trouble pronouncing Kwame's name, stumbling over it in a terribly comical way each time. To make it easier for him and honour his friendship with him, Kwame decided that he would go by the name 'John'. He only used that name in England, however, because he did not want to forget his true identity.

Unsurprisingly, Kwame had brought his trusty trumpet along to England, and would play for his father and their hosts nearly every evening after dinner. John and Pat were spellbound by the seventh note, and never failed to tell anyone who wished to hear that they knew the most talented teen from West Africa. Their consistent praise drew people from far and wide to hear Kwame play.

One morning, John let out an unseemly shriek, staring down at a folded sheet of parchment. Kwame, Nana, and Pat rushed over, wondering what the fuss was about. They looked down, and froze. The letter bore the royal seal of King Henry VII. Opening the letter with shaky hands, John read its contents aloud. King Henry was in need of a new trumpeter, and had heard of Kwame's talent. Kwame was to be the King's guest in two weeks' time.

The two weeks seemed to crawl by, and Kwame spent nearly every minute of it worrying about his upcoming meeting with the King. What if the King hated his playing? What if the King could not see past his appearance? And what if the King did like his playing? What happened then?

As he took his first steps into the King's entertainment parlour, Kwame feared he would be sick. He was so nervous. But when he lifted his trumpet and began to play, the King, the Queen, and the royal courtiers disappeared. The only people that remained in the room were his father and John.

Almost as soon as it started, it was over. The last note hung in the air between Kwame and the King, still ringing faintly. Kwame lowered his trumpet and bowed. Thunderous applause – led by the King – jerked Kwame out of his formal bow in surprise. The King, the Queen, and the royal courtiers were clapping madly, nodding approvingly.

'Well done, young John,' said the King once the applause faded away. 'Well done.'

And so began the life of John Blanke, trumpeter to King Henry VII and later King Henry VIII.

Adelaide Damoah
Artist
Story edited by Ella Wu

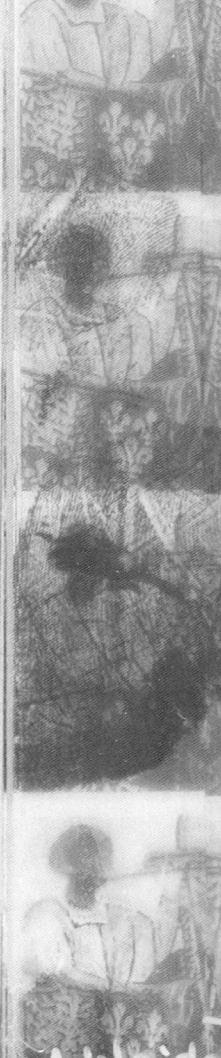

Adelaide Damoah, *John Blanke*,
295 × 210 × 13 mm, glass, card and ink

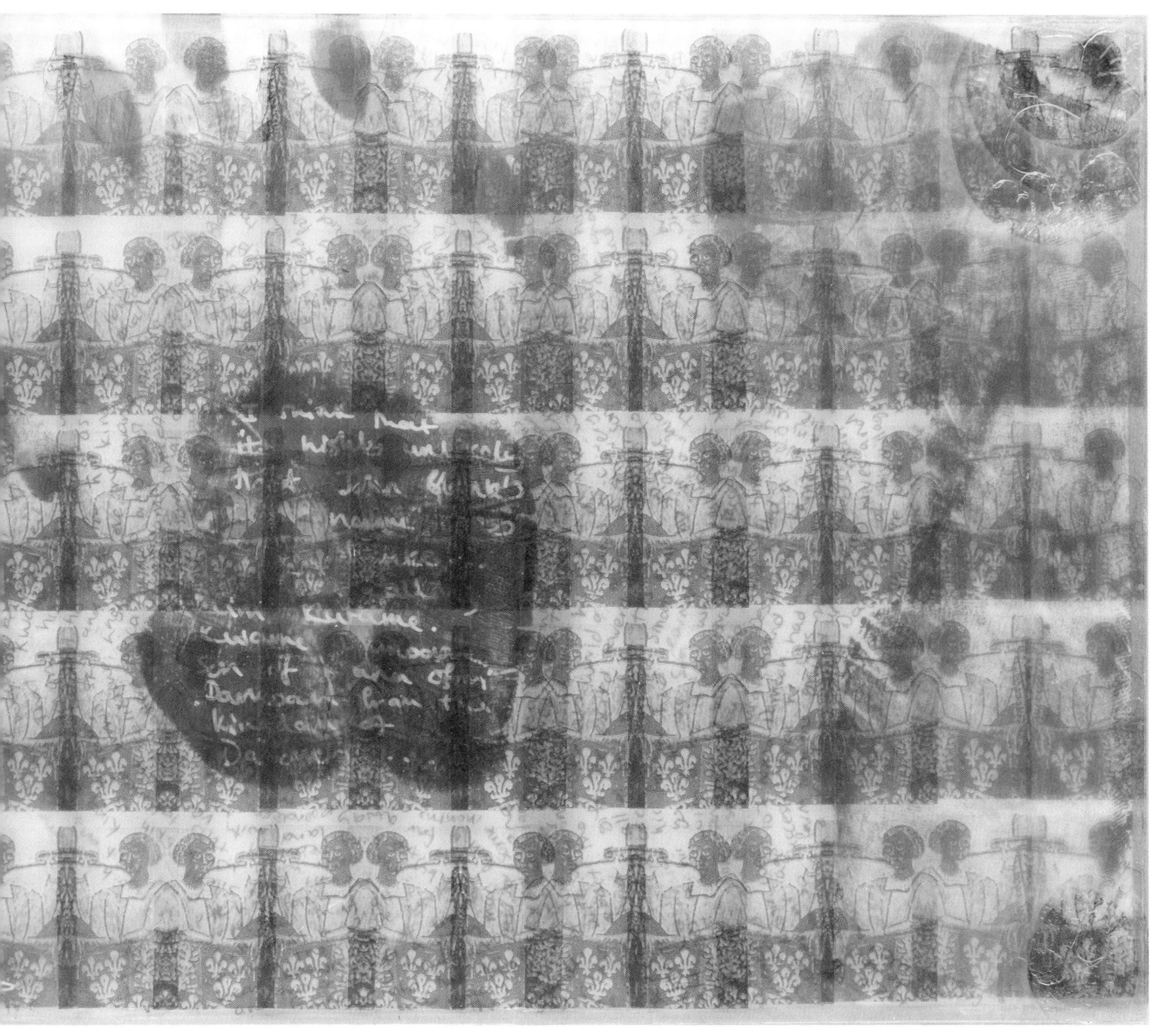

I imagined John Blanke as a 'trump card'. His status, as one of the earliest, visualised records of a Black person resident in England in the 16th century, stands as a definitive challenge and counterpoint to those who are yet to accept that the black historical presence on these shores pre-dates the 'Empire Windrush'. As with a deck of cards (symbolically denoting his place within the royal court of Henry VIII), John plays his hand impeccably. His purpose, as a trumpeter, sounding a clarion call to awake the historical, moral and social consciousness of this country, could not be clearer.

Jon Daniel
(1966-2017)
Independent. Creative Director. Designer.
Artist. Author. Curator. Collector

Jon Daniel (2020), *John Blanke*, 210 × 297 mm, digital print on parchment

'Henry's trumpeter, whose black face refuses to be washed out of history'

Professor Nandini Das
Professor of Early Modern English Literature and Culture

If you were of child in 16th century Europe, you would probably be familiar with the Adagia, a huge collection of proverbs put together by one of the greatest scholars of the period – the Dutch humanist, Desiderius Erasmus. From its first appearance in 1500, its pages were full of pithy little sayings and memorable words of advice, handy both for its wisdom and useful bite-sized snippets of Latin practice for new learners, and among them you would find two reminders.

The first appeared in a list of tasks that were impossible to achieve. 'Aethiopem lavas; aethiopem dealbas,' it remonstrated. 'You are washing or making the Ethiopian white.' In a later 1508 edition, Erasmus would add a note to explain: 'that inborn blackness of the Ethiopian, which Pliny thinks to be a result of heat from the nearness of the sun, cannot be washed away with water not whitened by any means whatever.' For Erasmus, it is a useful image for other impossible tasks – like praising someone who does not deserve praise, or teaching one who cannot be taught. For the second, 'Aethiops non albescit' ('An Ethiopian cannot be whitened'), he explained, 'This is usually said of those who will never change their nature.' Erasmus traced its source back to one of Aesop's fables, about a man who bought a black slave and tried to wash him clean, 'leaving him ill, as well as coloured no better than before'.

Erasmus was not the only one to use this image, or these associations. You would find it in the Bible: 'Can the black Moor change his skin? or the leopard his spots?' was the rhetorical question posed in Jeremiah 13.23, because those 'that are accustomed to do evil' cannot be expected to do any good. No wonder both Aesop's fable and the idea of 'washing the Ethiope' became popular topics for moral illustrations and mottos throughout the sixteenth century across Europe: countless variations of a black man being scrubbed by the Europeans surrounding him, an example of folly and the impossible.

Erasmus first met the future Henry VIII in 1499, the year before the Adagia first emerged in print, when Henry was a precocious and impressionable eight-year-old prince. Over the next decades, Erasmus would visit England often. He was in England from 1509-1514, when John Blanke made his appearance in the Westminster Tournament Roll of 1511. It is tempting to imagine their paths crossing – the humanist scholar for whom 'the Ethiope' had featured simply as a convenient, accepted metaphor, and Henry's trumpeter, whose black face refuses to be washed out of history, his very survival in historical records acting both as a reminder of, and a challenge to, all those European assumptions about blackness and black skin.

Professor Nandini Das

For sources see page 259

I imagined John Blanke as a survivor who encountered ridicule, enmity and strife in his lifetime. Yet he succeeded as a court musician to the king. As such he was a testament to African achievement in an environment of severe challenge and exclusion.

Paul Dash
Artist

Paul Dash (2015) *John Blanke*, 210 × 297 mm, ink on paper

I imagined John Blanke as representing themes of the highest importance in world history: interaction and connectivity. Where did he come from? How did he get here? In what other ways did Africans collaborate with an expansionary Renaissance Europe? I discuss these themes in more detail in my historian page (page 80).

Phil Day
Rapper Historian

John Blanke's presence in Tudor England
Extract from Rap History of the World

So, I was in Bermuda
When I heard this rumour
About the Black Tudor
Pahrumphing his trumpet for the ruler
Henry VIII, in 1511,
Only nineteen, just
Two years he'd been
King and he was keen
On the Tournament
Got my instrument

Hurray my big day
Flag unfurled
Hair straight not curled
On my trusty nag
And hanging below my elbow
My proud handbag

So which one's John Blanke?
Middle column, second rank.
You mean the one mister
With the five Shakespeare Sisters?
He's persisted in history
And poses a couple of mysteries
Where's he from, what's his game?
What do we know apart from his name?
What do they think, his peers
How did he get here?
Four centuries before the Windrush Year?

Was he a beat-rocking Moroccan
Walking and talking in his turban
Maghrabian and urban
Or Sub-Saharan, West African
I asked Dr. Kaufmann
She said, well
"It remains a question mark,
But he does look quite dark"

© 2017 Phil Day

'The stories of John Blanke, and other Black Tudors, suggest that 16th century England was indifferent to skin colour racial difference'

Phil Day
Rapper Historian

John Blanke: Illustrative of Europe's Expanding Connectivity

The presence of a black musician at the English royal court in 1511 is illustrative of Europe's expanding connectivity with the rest of the world at that time. Some Africans in Dr Miranda Kaufmann's book *Black Tudors* (Kaufmann, 2017) travelled directly from West Africa, some via the Maghreb, Iberia and the Caribbean.

Contacts between societies in history had various motives – exploration, migration, trade, war, proselytization – and led to various forms of exchange – goods, technologies, ideas, religions, diseases, crops, etc – that drive change in history. The agricultural revolution 10,000 years ago in the Middle East, and the scientific/industrial revolutions since 1500 centred on Europe, both occurred in times and places of exceptional connectivity (Christian, 2004). These are central arguments of the *Rap History of the World* (Day, 2013).

Africans made important contributions to Europe's expansion. The production by African slave labour in the Americas of key inputs of the Industrial Revolution such as sugar and cotton is well known. But free and unfree African labour was also vital in American colonial societies – in food production, trades, shipbuilding, navigation, translation, military, and more (Kamen 2003, Davis 2006).

Other transatlantic migrants included disease organisms. First, Europeans brought a host of Old World diseases which devastated Amerindian populations. From the 1640s, African mosquitos established malaria and yellow fever; henceforth, only African labour could survive in Caribbean environments (McNeill, J.R. 2010, Day 2017). European-indentured labour ended, slavery became linked exclusively with race, and race stigmatised.

The stories of John Blanke, and other Black Tudors, suggest that 16th century England was indifferent to skin colour racial difference, also that slavery was considered wrong on principle. Given what followed, we are struck by the non-linearity of the history of 'progressive' ideas and humanist moral values. We need better explanations for their rise and decline.

Finally, as a skilled artisan, JB reminds of the neglected history of African civilizations; the Mali Empire was the largest of the Sahelian Kingdoms which flourished c9th-16th centuries. These featured considerable sophistication including trade, town, cities, literacy, taxation, armies, and administration.

Phil Day

For sources see page 259

I imagined John Blanke as having a strong sense of determination, perhaps quite fearless. As well as being skilled, he must have been charismatic, too – somebody who put people at ease. He was probably fluent in at least two European languages, but I wonder if he gave much thought to, or had ever even seen, his African ancestral homeland?

Kimathi Donkor
Artist

Kimathi Donkor (2016), *John Blanke,* 230 × 310 mm, water colour and ink on Arches Aquarelle paper

'[John Blanke] the First Black Person In British History With A Name And A Portrait'

J Draper
Tour guide and London history nerd

@JDraper on YouTube

 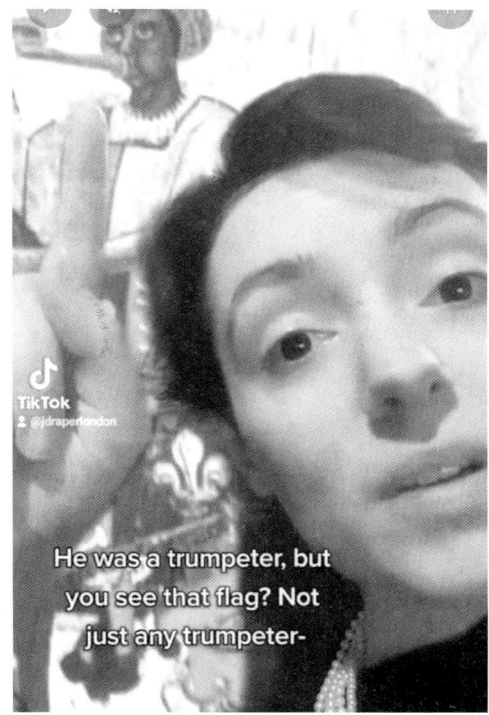 
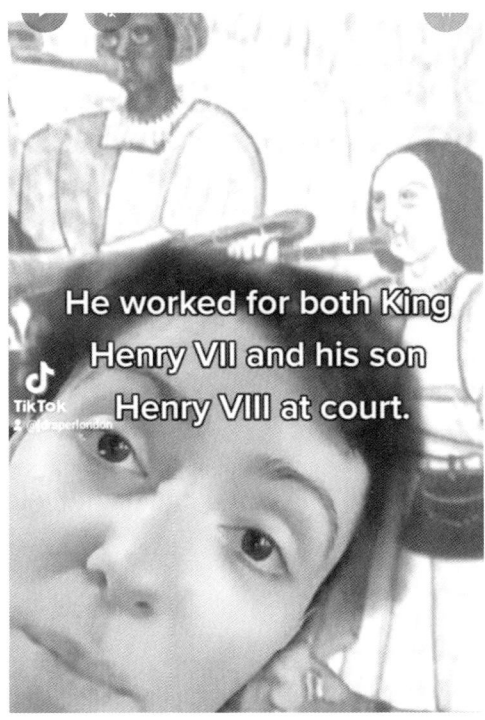  

I imagined John Blanke as a talented career musician and a popular personality. He was a confident man, a traveller and a dedicated practitioner.

I imagine Blanke's life would have been a very interesting tale of his origins and his life experiences which led to a period of life in England as trumpeter who rose in the ranks of his orchestra to be a mainstay at King Henry VIII's court.

No doubt Blanke was very much a curiosity but that he was equally as curious about the natives and felt accepted and settled, probably some charm and wit to complement the novelty of being an exotic foreigner.

My picture shows him feeling casual after he has performed and dismounted, party to his own thoughts as the Tudor world he inhabits marvels at John Blanke.

Mengistu Etim
Freelance Caricaturist and Illustrator

Mengistu Etim (2022), *John Blanke*, 210 × 290 mm, digital print

I imagined John Blanke as a powerful force of sound. Heard through all the pageantry and the sound of horses' hooves, heard throughout history and remembered as much for his resounding sound as his resourceful and enduring race. Kings of old cherished his sound, which heralded the arrival of confident crowns to render them history's immortals. To us, the silence of his sound rendered by history continues to be deafening.

Graeme Mortimer Evelyn
Artist

Graeme Mortimer Evelyn (2016), *John Blank*e, 210 × 290 mm, ink on paper

I imagine John Blanke as a musical prodigy. A man gifted with the instinctual knowledge and ability to make beautiful sounds from any instrument he touches. A man with rhythm woven into his being.

Tinuke Fagborun
Artist

Tinuke Fagborun (2020) *John Blanke*, 206 × 297mm, digital illustration

I imagined John Blanke as a cheerful fellow, bringing smiles to faces with his fanfares and tunes. He was paid for his passion – playing the trumpet, which he would do with equal relish every day, whether it was for one man in a back room or hundreds at a royal tournament.

Dan Farrimond
Multimedia artist

Dan Farrimond (2016) *John Blanke*, 210 × 290 mm, digital print

12 February 1511

THE WESTMINSTER TOURNAMENT CHALLENGE

A challenge to noble knights Ceure Loyall, Vailliaunt Desyre, Bone Voloyr and Joyous Panser to accomplish certain feates of Armes in honour of the birth of a young prince to King Henry and Queen Catherine.

I imagined John Blanke as a thoughtful and insightful musician who observed new cultures and learned languages as he played in Royal Courts across Europe. He sounded the trumpet not only to herald the King but also as a proclamation of his own liberty. With the timeless language of music he transcended barriers of race and status. He was heard and understood.

Jenny Fay
Artist

I am John Blanke
Now you see me
Philosopher
Poet
Linguist
Musician
A man of the Renaissance
A Renaissance Man

Captured for the King
It is he who is captivated now
I speak to him
In language that transcends
All barriers of space, of race, of culture,
of time
I speak to him in the language of music

I play a fanfare for the infant prince
I play him a lullaby
I play a song of loss
I play in remembrance

Do you hear the loudest sound of the trumpet?
The silence after the last note fades?

I give you that silence

I am John Blanke
Now you see me

© Jenny Fay 2024

Jenny Fay (2016) *John Blanke*,
297 × 210 mm, charcoal on paper

'Trumpets were expected to have a good voice as well as to be able to sound the fanfares'

Professor Catherine Fletcher
Professor of History

John Blanke: the Tudor Roman Connection?

In 1585 Tommaso Garzoni published a guide to 'all the professions of the world'. Among them was that of 'trumpet' (or in Garzoni's Italian trombetta). The role he described was analogous to the English herald or town-crier, someone who might play fanfares and make official announcements. Of course, a trumpet like John Blanke might have had considerable musical skill as well, but that wasn't the main function of the job. It was often more mundane.

Standing in the town he might have to proclaim royal decrees, taxes, trials or executions. In a society where many people couldn't read, this role was vital to get the authorities' announcements out. Trumpets were expected to have a good voice as well as to be able to sound the fanfares that drew the crowds to hear them, but we can only speculate on John Blanke's tone.

Garzoni found plenty of precedents for the modern role of trumpet in sources from ancient Greece and Rome. In T*he Iliad* Homer attributed to one trumpet, Stentor, a voice of iron and the volume of fifty men. From Stentor comes the word 'stentorian' to describe a loud or powerful tone.

Another Greek trumpet, Achia, won three Olympiads and was commemorated with a statue. Cicero's cases, too, provided evidence. In a speech against the trumpet Sextus Naevius, who had a dispute with Cicero's client Publius Quintius, Cicero attacked Naevius as a buffoon. But his words also reveal that Naevius was a freedman, and Garzoni picked up this point to emphasise that ancient trumpets had been free and not enslaved.

It's a fascinating observation in light of what we know about John Blanke's free status, and also what we know about the Africans who came to Britain with the Roman army. Perhaps some of them were trumpets too.

Professor Catherine Fletcher

I imagined John Blanke as a strong, charismatic, creative, black man making his mark on the world – whilst carrying his culture and heritage on his shoulders with pride.

I feel my son Dean has these same qualities so I used his image in a scraperboard etching to represent John Blanke, with Adinkra symbols adorning his shoulders.

I chose to use Adinkra symbols as their purpose is to visually communicate concepts or original thoughts.

Whilst making the etching and scratching into the board I felt the connection between John Blanke's pride and heritage and that of my sons.

Sharon Foster
Artist, Illustrator, Curator

Adinkrahene
symbol of greatness, charisma and leadership

Dwennimmen
symbol of humility, together with strength

Nkyinkyim
symbol of initiative, dynamism and versatility

Sharon Foster (2022) *John Blanke*, 210 × 297 mm, scraperboard etching

**From John Blanke to Wynton Marsalis
A Continuum of Great Masters: 16th - 21st Century**

I imagined John Blanke as the man who blew a medieval fanfare that echoed down through to the 20th century jazz era and continues to the classical players of the 21st century.

Fowokan
Artist

Fowokan (2016) *John Blanke*, 210 × 290 mm, digital image

I imagined John Blanke as a man who might have felt he was a stranger in many strange lands. He would perform for a king and petition the king for backdated pay. He would also marry and have a life with his new bride.

A robust and confident man – there are facets of John Blanke in all of us.

Brian Francis
Artist

Brian Francis (2017) *John Blanke*,
200 × 252 mm, graphite pencil on canvas

'I would like to think he once sat for a portrait dressed in his best turban, gifted violet gown, with a trumpet by his side'

Kendall Francis
Assistant Paintings Conservator

A Portrait of an Unknown Black Man

A *Portrait of an Unknown Black Man*, *A Portrait of an Unknown Moor*, *A Portrait of an Unknown African*, *A Portrait of an Unknown Negro*.

On reflection, the earliest painted portraits with these titles and sole individuals include, and are limited to, *Portrait of an African Man (Christophle le more?)* c.1525, *Portrait of a Wealthy African* c.1530, *Portrait of an unknown African woman holding a clock* c.1580.

It is obvious that the presence of John Blanke to be distinguished as a named individual and as a black man on the Westminster Tournament Roll is of great significance and a distinct choice by the artist/workshop during the planning stage. During the 16th century, particularly in the court of Henry VIII, there was significant political importance for portraiture in Europe depicting monarchs, nobility, and courtiers. European artists flocked to London as this trend grew and became even more fashionable and affordable as the century continued, resulting in portraits of merchants, wives, and children. Considering this value on portraiture, John Blanke's 'individualism' and his respected position as trumpeter to Henry VIII, I would like to think he once sat for a portrait dressed in his best turban, gifted violet gown, with a trumpet by his side.

But what happened to this portrait of John and of his other black contemporaries? The two depictions of John have lasted on The Roll most likely due to its high status and the fact that 99.9% of people depicted are white nobility/royalty. A conceivable reason why a potential painted portrait of John Blanke did not survive is due to the historical trends of restoration and collecting, both influenced by changing political and social climates.

Like the whitewashing of history which has destroyed and disregarded different cultures, ethnic identities, and diverse communities to propel white dominant privilege, so too has the tradition of conservation and the collecting of art works. Restorers and art collectors for centuries have been important stakeholders in preserving our heritage. They hold special positions determining and upholding what society considers valuable, priority and worth promoting for current communities and future generations. The transatlantic slave trade began towards the end of the 16th century and it was integral to racialise, dehumanise and barbarise black and brown people to the point where most artefacts, collections and institutions are still charged with these legacies of slavery, colonialism, white supremacism and systemic racism which propel the 'racial superiority' of white people. These decisions by homogeneously white collectors and restorers had and still have a great impact on society, on our cultural heritage and accurate history which is predominantly still presented to a white audience. So, for the purpose of maintaining and defending a system of wealth, privilege and power for white people, artworks like the proposed portrait of a prominent, talented black man may have purposefully not been chosen to preserve or collect, been left to degrade, or been damaged or destroyed to dull the aspirations and hope of a whole community of people continuously denied their positive and influential history.

The optimistic conservator in me wants to believe that maybe one day someone might discover, while clearing a deserted basement, an old damaged Portrait of an Unknown Black Man wearing a turban, draped in a gown of violet cloth, holding a trumpet. For the meantime, some of the artists' contributions in the John Blanke Project may inadvertently be re-imaging this 'lost' artwork; so, for now our acknowledgment, imaginings and interpretations of Black British figures are enough.

Kendall Francis

For sources see page 259

I imagined John Blanke as a talented, proud yet sad man, surrounded by and filled with love for his wife, his queen, his music. But it wasn't enough.

Dr Djibril Diallo, Senior Advisor to the Executive Director UNAIDS has said:

> *They [African (im)migrants living in Europe or the US or anywhere outside their countries] will wake up physically in those countries but, mentally and emotionally, they wake up every morning in their countries of origin.*

Kadija George
Poet

The Mysterious Demise of John Blanke
(after Jean Passerat's "Villanelle," or "J'ay perdu ma tourterelle")
By Kadija Sesay

A Broken Heart Killed John Blanke
My Gentle Husband, My Love
Vicious Rumors Played A Prank

Mortified, My Blackbird Drank
In Despair, One Tiny Shove
A Broken Heart Killed John Blanke

To See Him Weep, My Heart Sank
Honoured To Wear The White Glove
Vicious Rumours Played A Prank

My Trumpeteer, Raised In Rank
By His Queen, A Cut Above…
A Broken Heart Killed John Blanke
I Found Him Dead, Struck Point blank
Such Tears, My Loss Undreamed Of
Vicious Rumours Played A Prank

John Was True and John Was Frank
For Ever, His Ladylove
A Broken Heart, Killed John Blanke
Vicious Rumours Played A Prank.

© Kadija Sesay, 2015

I imagined John Blanke as a confident and assertive character, a free agent, and a man of standing. Ultimately, however, he remains for me an unknowable individual. We can register his movements in the courts of Henry VIII as one narrative thread amongst others, a hairline trace that signals towards further, more hidden, histories of black people in Britain in this period.

Holly Graham
Artist

Holly Graham (2017) *John Blanke*, 210 × 296 mm, folded digital inkjet print on paper, card

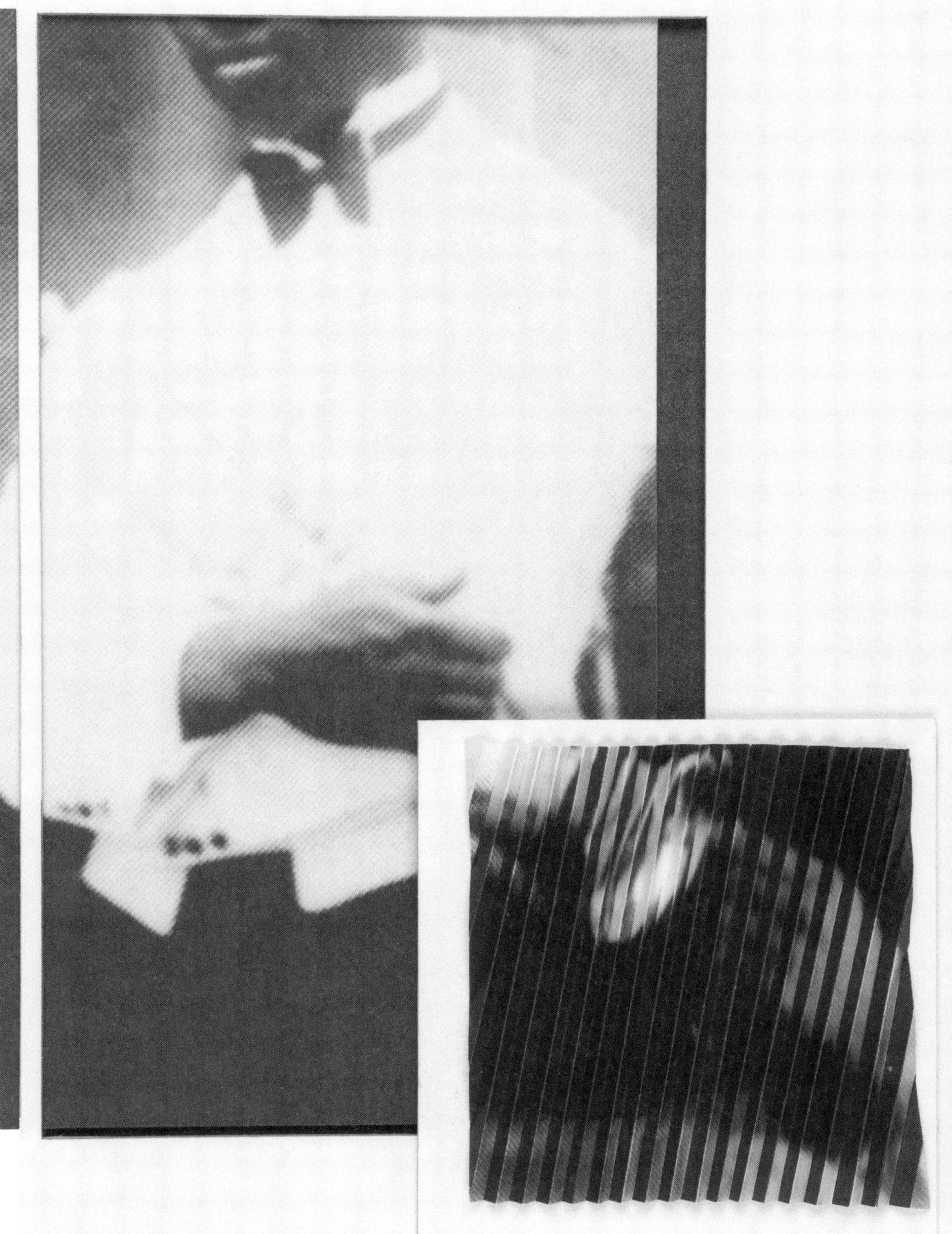

'an intriguing challenge to historians'

Jeffrey Green
Historian

John Blanke: an Intriguing Challenge to Historians.

Until photography and the inexpensive Kodak camera, there were few images of most Britons. Paintings and sculpture were long dominated by the Christian church. Later secular portrait paintings were financed by patrons who flaunted their wealth and status by occasionally including servants – some were black. Images of black Britons who are named and whose lives have been traced are rare. In some cases – the man sometimes thought to be Olaudah Equiano, in the Albert Memorial Museum in Exeter, for example – there are doubts about identity, and the Reynolds' portrait of Francis Barber of 1767 is not supported by evidence. The case of John Blanke is clearer and earlier.

He is pictured in an early 16th century manuscript, and is mentioned in royal court documents. King Henry VIII paid for Blanke's wedding clothes in 1512.

There are earlier images but not in England – with the 13th century statue of St Maurice in Magdeburg cathedral in Saxony (eastern Germany) being just one of many located in Germany. There are fleeting glimpses and images in Britain, such as the bowls of tobacco pipes carved as Africans and the use of 'Black Boy' as a name for ale houses or pubs (there were two in Tottenham, London, in 1690) but long after John Blanke. The East Sussex hamlet of Blackboys is thought to have that name from the now-extinct charcoal industry, and the Atlantic slave trade led to African images on coats of arms such as John Hawkins (died 1595).

Blanke's presence suggests other black people, not working for the English monarchs, and like the mass of Britons, obscure, were out and about 500 years ago. It is an intriguing challenge to historians.

Jeffery Green

For sources see page 259

I imagined John Blank as the trumpeter at work with his colleagues as presented on the tapestry. Outside the frame, he is also a son, brother, and father living an everyday life of the period with his family and friends not far from the Thames. The tapestry is a contemporary photograph of the time, where the greater part of life with its dramas goes on well outside the frame.

Joy Gregory
Artist working with photography and related media

Joy Gregory (2017) *John Blanke*, 210 × 297, process description: inkjet print on archival paper based on a gum print of a drawing depicting a trumpet made using hand-ground charcoal as a pigment in 2017

I imagined John Blanke as a very talented musician. He was also a person who recognised his own talent and value. He wasn't shy of speaking up for what he believed in and I think he therefore led a very interesting and rewarding life, as well as leading the way for others to recognise their professional value.

Annis Harrison
Artist

Annis Harrison (2019). *John Blanke*
280 × 355 mm, oil on canvas

I imagined John Blanke as a man of courage and some measure of determination in creating for himself a life and a living of high status within a culture that holds his countrymen in contempt. I admire his intellect, and the prudence that he must have refined in order to thrive, to prosper and even to remain safe and a free man.

I imagine John Blanke a brother.

Valda Jackson
Artist

Valda Jackson (2016) *John Blanke*, 210 × 300 mm, pencil and ink on board

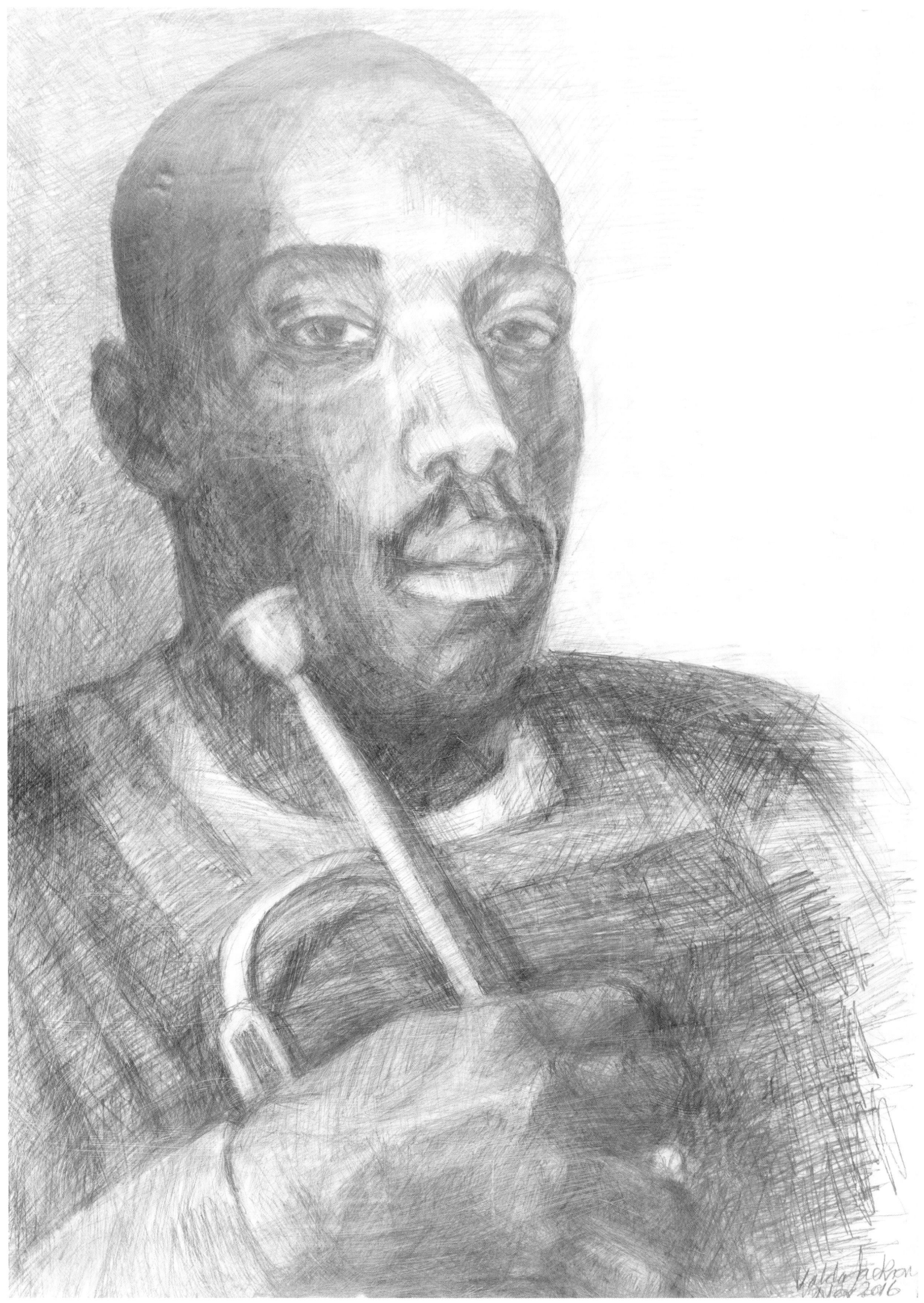

'[John Blanke] had a female contemporary at the Tudor court ... It is a tantalising prospect that [they] may have met'

Lauren Johnson
Historian, Author and Heritage Interpreter

John Blanke Had a Female Contemporary at the Tudor Court

For decades, Catalina of Motril suffered from a false attribution. Since the 19th century, when the Marques de Molins transcribed Spanish archival material, it was known that a woman called Catalina was the bedchamber servant and 'once the slave' of Catherine of Aragon. Catalina attended on her mistress during Catherine's brief marriage to Prince Arthur of England (1501-2). As the woman who removed the sheets from Catherine's marital bed, Catalina could have borne witness to one of History's most enduring mysteries: did Catherine and Arthur consummate their marriage?

After Arthur's death, both Catherine and Catalina remained in England and Catalina's later life can be traced through contemporary Spanish state papers. In 1509, she witnessed the second marriage of her mistress Catherine, to Arthur's younger brother, Henry VIII. Like John Blanke (who it has been suggested entered England via Spanish service) Catalina may have made her way from Catherine's household to the royal court. It is a tantalising prospect that John and Catalina may have met there and conversed. What experiences might they have shared? Of displacement, of 'othering' by contemporary commentators (Thomas More has left a particularly insensitive comment on the black attendants of Catherine of Aragon) and of making a home in a new country?

Whereas John married in England, Catalina left at some point before 1526 and returned to Spain, where she married a crossbow-maker called Oviedo. To travel and marry freely, her enslavement must have been considered at an end. Catalina had two children with Oviedo before being widowed, then returned to her hometown of Motril in Granada. It was while she lived there that she re-emerged on the political scene, sought as an unusually 'well-informed' witness during Catherine of Aragon's divorce proceedings. Henry VIII insisted his marriage to Catherine was invalidated by her previous relationship with Arthur. Catalina knew whether it had been a 'true marriage' or – as Catherine insisted – it had not. But whether she was found to testify, we do not know.

But Molins made a fundamental error, which has been repeated ever since (most recently in the Spanish Princess series on Starz): he conflated the enslaved Catalina with 'Catalina de Cardones', the dueña of Catherine of Aragon's household. Cardones was high born and it is enticing to consider that the enslaved Catalina was once an aristocrat. But Cardones returned to Spain before 1509, and is extremely unlikely to have married a lowly crossbow-maker. In fact, 'Catalina of Motril' (as I call her) was unnamed in Molins' account for 1501, simply one of two enslaved women at the bottom of the list of Catherine's servants. Indeed, her name may not originally have been Catalina. Those enslaved in Spain were often made to assume the name of their 'owner' – in Spanish, Catherine of Aragon was 'la Infanta Catalina'.

Lauren Johnson

For sources see page 259

I imagined John Blanke as a talented man in his own right, enough talent to catch the attention of the most powerful king England ever had.

Tam Joseph
Artist

Tam Joseph (2017) *John Blanke*, 210 × 297 mm, ink on paper

I imagined John Blanke as a courageous and resilient creative who chose the timeless medium of graffiti to capture his presence as an African in the European Royal Court for future generations to unearth.

I reimagine his skilful use of language, both written and spoken in my freestyle *calligrafffiti* artwork. Through the beautiful script he proudly declares: *I was here, and I was exceptional!*

Linett Kamala
Artist and Educator

Linett Kamala (2018) *John Blanke*, 210 × 297 mm, mixed media

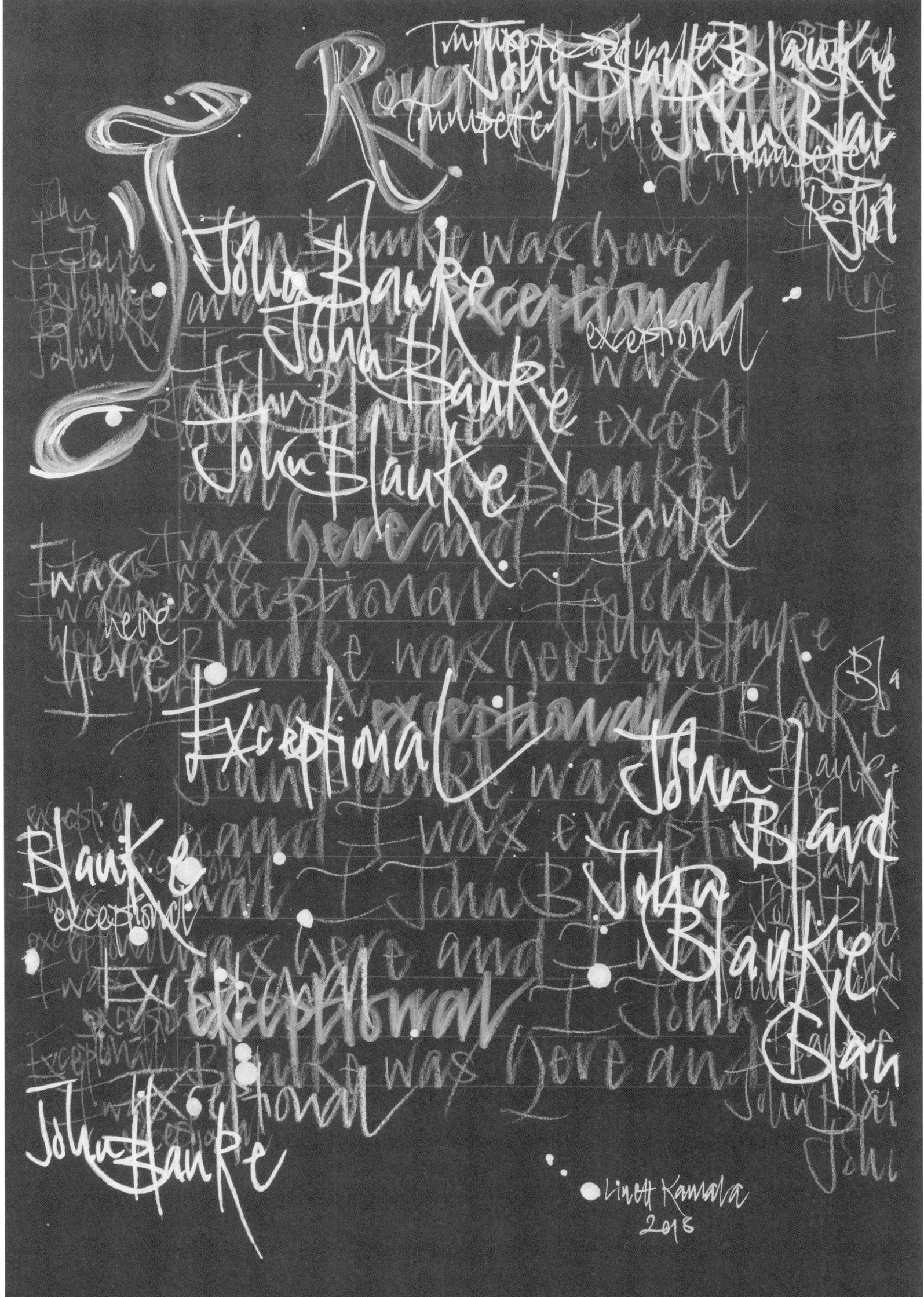

'John Blanke's name [is] part of a broad, enduring European phenomenon'

Paul Kaplan
Professor of Art History

John Blanke and his Afro-European Namesakes

John Blanke is an important figure in the early history of the sub-Saharan diaspora in Europe, because he had a skilled position in royal service and because we have both clear textual and clear visual evidence about him. The very fact that we know his name seems significant, though there is the paradox that 'blank' also implies a void.

His name, however, links him to a series of other Africans, both real and imagined, from the 1300s to the 1600s. John Blanke is a nickname, of a type known as an antiphrasis, which means that a person is identified by his opposite, like Robin Hood's huge comrade, Little John; Blanke in this context means white (as 'blanc' in French).

Dark-skinned people were already ironically referred to as white or silver in ancient Rome, and in 1354 the King of Aragon made the gift of an enslaved black African called 'Johan Blanc' to King John the Good of France. Here the Christian name was meant to flatter the French king. In 1495, closer to John Blanke's time, one 'Zuan Bianco,' also called John the Ethiopian, was identified as a valiant commander of infantry in the Venetian army, and after his death in battle the Venetian state awarded a generous pension to his wife and children. ('Zuan' is Venetian dialect for John, and 'bianco' is Italian for white.) Shakespeare may indirectly have drawn on Zuan Bianco in conceiveing his own black Venetian commander, Othello.

A bit later, in 1638, the Spaniard Andres de Claramonte wrote a play called *The Valiant Black in Flanders,* with another courageous African soldier as the protagonist. This man is another John (Juan), who is eventually granted the last name of the army's leader, the Duke of Alba, thus becoming Juan Alba – and, in Latin, 'alba' means white.

All this means we must consider John Blanke's name as part of a broad, enduring European phenomenon, though it does not make the 'blacke trumpet' any less of an individual.

Paul Kaplan

I imagined John Blanke as a learned man with a greater awareness of the world. A note from John Blanke's diary:

I commissioned this portrait from the sum I was entitled to from my petition, to adorn the wall of my modest reading room. Although it cost a tidy sum and against my wife's judgment, I felt it important to indulge in such a venture. Not so for myself, but as a recorded note in this year 1513, that others may know in future generations. That others of my race know that an African held such a position. I sleep this night satisfied having made my way in a land far from my origin through struggle but with some success.

Alvin Kofi
Artist

Alvin Kofi (2015) *John Blanke*,
210 × 297 mm, pencil on paper

I imagined John Blanke as an adept trumpeter who was underpaid for his services. My portrait hones in on Blanke's fluency and the trumpet chords, syncopation and riffs he must have privately practised daily. John Blanke would have warmed up on his instrument before performing at the royal courts. How did he play to tune up for his official repertoire and duties?

Atta Kwami
(1956-2021)
Artist

Atta Kwami (2019) *John Blanke*, 210 × 300 mm, acrylic on handmade paper

I imagined John Blanke as an aristocrat, a socialite and a nobleman of great repute. In my mind's eye, I pictured him to have drawn crowds which he entertained as an artiste of the royal court. Much more also as a person of dual identity and nationality.

Wole Lagunju
Artist

Wole Lagunju (2019) *John Blanke*, 225 × 305 mm, inks on paper

'[John Blanke] was not "too ambitious", nor did he have "unrealistic expectations"'

Renée Landell
Researcher, Writer, Speaker and Activist

John Blanke's tenacity is shared among many Black Brits fighting for equitable pay and other workers' rights today

Today, the struggle for equitable pay and promotion is widespread among Black workers in Britain. However, it is worth reflecting on the contemporary significance of John Blanke, the renowned Black Tudor, who successfully convinced a King to approve his petition.

When a more senior trumpeter, an Italian man named Domynck Justinian, died Blanke began to reconsider his own contributions and the worth of his labour. In a petition, he writes: 'It may therefore please your Highness in consideration of the true & faithful service which your servant daily doeth [...] to give and grant unto him the same room [position] of Trumpet which Dominic deceased late had'. Blanke's daily wage (8d.) was not considered inequitable by any means and he was already playing in royal courts. But his determination, which is shared among many talented Black workers today, resulted in his promotion to a more senior rank and the doubling of his wage (16d. per day).

According to a 2022 report by the Living Wage Foundation, 'the ongoing cost of the living crisis means those in insecure and low-paid jobs are struggling more than ever before. However, it is minority ethnic workers who are disproportionately paid the lowest wages in the UK who are being hit the hardest.' Chattel slavery saw the unethical free labour of Africans across the Atlantic, and today racial injustices in the workforce stand as a harrowing echo of the colonial economic system.

Hailing from a time that precedes the enslavement of African peoples, John Blanke stands as an example that Black people can be promoted to senior positions due to their merit. He was not 'too ambitious', nor did he have 'unrealistic expectations'; he was worthy like many Black Brits today who deserve to be compensated and rewarded fairly for their contributions.

Renée Landell

For sources see page 259

'[John Blanke] a significant paradigm for how we can reconceptualise race by unlearning'

Vicky Lane
Senior Curator, Art and Identity
Royal Museums Greenwich

John Blanke: Taking a portrait out of Henry VIII's Roll

Sometimes the archive forces us to 'unlearn' history. The rediscovery of John Blanke represents a significant paradigm for how we can reconceptualise race by unlearning.

This unlearning has a vital urgency because it questions the history which has been written on top of John Blanke; the layers of whiteness which have constructed a particular lens to view him through. This encompasses the introduction and legacies of the 1661 Slave Code, known as *An Act for Better Ordering and Governing of Negroes*, which legalised racial violence and a systematic negation of the human rights of black people by reducing them to 'chattel'. This was reinforced by the scientific racism of the Enlightenment and British Imperialism which normalised the inequalities and violences of systemic racism we still witness today. Through unlearning, we can see the white supremacist, colonialist logic which underlies this: financial exploitation and gain.

If John Blanke was just a name in Henry VIII's accounts, he wouldn't have the same impact. It is his visual incarnation through art which marks his difference. Although represented in a schematic manner (which has been reimagined evocatively through the artists in this project), he is distinguished by his skin colour and dress, indicating an early 16th century perspective and necessity to represent and respect his individuality. A distinctive shift in the black presence in the art of the North Atlantic occurs from the early 17th century to the mid-20th century. In this period, black people are largely reduced to caricature, representations of oppression and subservience or are defined by their absence.

Beyond disrupting the view of the English as ethnically undifferentiated in 1511, John Blanke's portraits produce a new discourse which contradict such epistemic cultural forms by positioning him as an equal in Tudor England. Although nobody can know if John suffered racism, his image, success and equality in pay for his expertise and skills points to a different vision of race than that inscribed by the transatlantic trade in enslaved Africans (still worryingly embedded in the ethnicity pay gaps of today).

He provides a new liberatory framework for positioning a shared language of change. As Michael Ohajuru has stated, the pronouns we should be using for working on British history are: 'we/us, our/ours'. It is essential we all take on this entangled history and use John Blanke's portraits as a means of unlearning together.

Vicky Lane

©Vicky Lane

I imagined John Blanke as, or his family as, commissioning a yard of cloth for his travels – either before he left West Africa or in celebration on returning home. (I know we are not sure about that part.) The cloth acts as an emotional trigger, a cultural reference, a messenger of life and a substitute for cultural memory.

Dee Lawrence
Visual Artist

Dee Lawrence (2020) *John's Celebratory Cloth*, 260 × 315 mm, textile

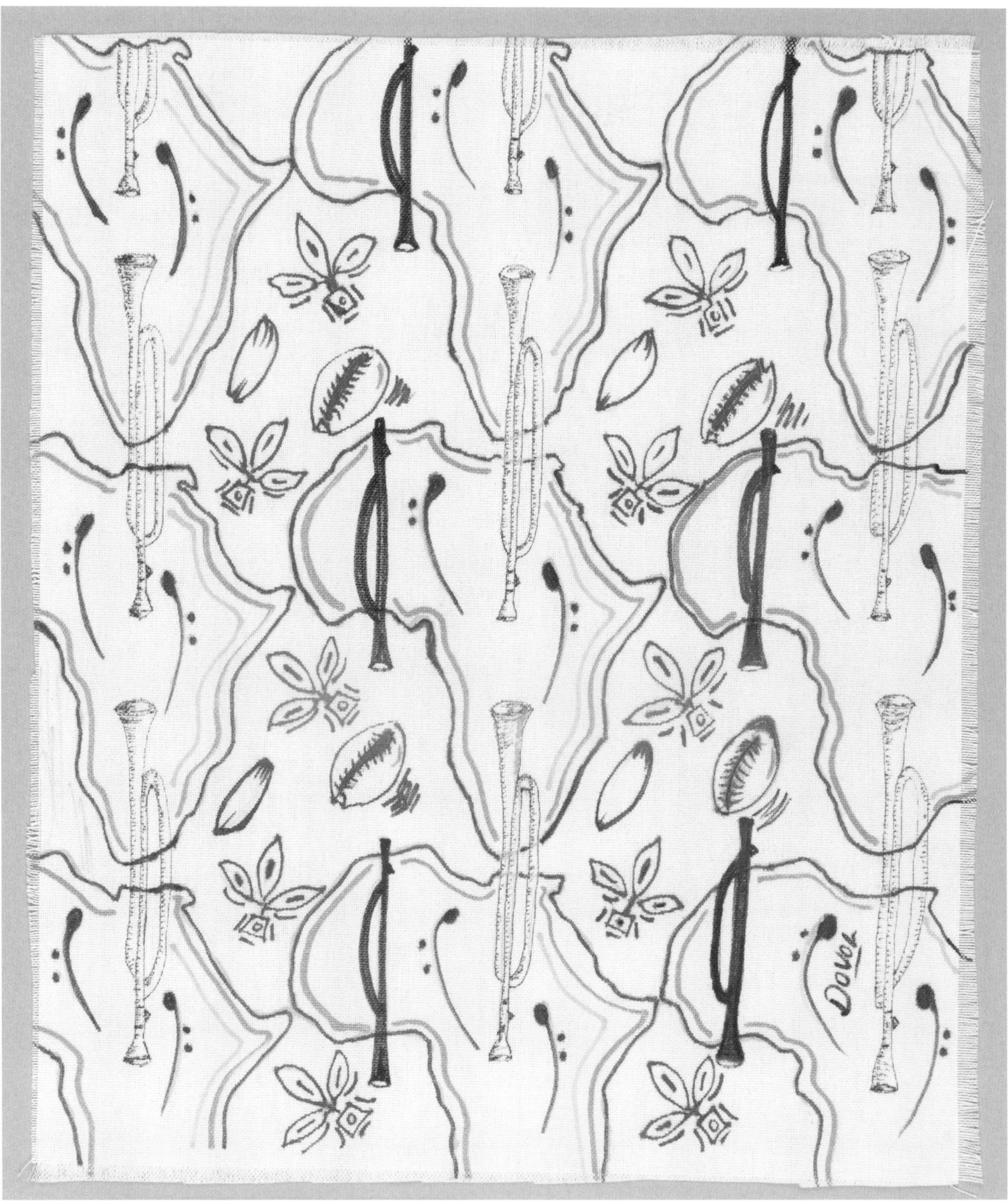

I imagined John Blanke as a prominent person within the Royal pageantry. A man who gained high accolades to reach his way to the top. Most probably coming from humble beginnings to becoming a recognised figure. A strong-minded and disciplined man, who probably had to face a lot of discrimination throughout the succession of his life.

Jason Lee
Illustrator

Jason Lee (2023) *John Blanke*,
285 × 210 mm, pencil and paper

'[John Blanke] open[s] a space of experience towards transformations of knowledge, history an experience of race, self, and community'

Serena Lee
Associate Lecturer of Contextual Studies

An Adorned Black Trumpeter Encapsulated in Posterity

The shrill trump, the spirit-stirring drum
Othello, Shakespeare (1603)

Hark ye John Blanke!

John Blanke, a Tudor royal trumpeter, is pictured as an integral part of King Henry the IIIV's procession. Hand on hip and cheeks puffed out, an adorned Black trumpeter encapsulated in posterity. A grand parade was a regular occurrence to showcase the wealth and grandeur of the royal courts. His appearance pervades the traditional notion of Tudor Britain. The 1511 Westminster Tournament Roll is painted, almost 60 feet long and 14 3/4 inches wide. Blanke is a pillar, along with his fellow trumpeters, at the front and the back of the roll.

Blanke wears a white shirt under a knee-length two-tone, puff-sleeved tunic and a pair of scarlet red hosiery. However, unlike the other riders, he wears a jade green bonnet embroidered with illuminated gold thread in an elaborate pattern. In the Tudor period, individuals wore their wealth. The type of cloth they wore clearly signified social status. Sumptuary restrictions were placed on a range of fabrics including cloth of gold, velvet, silks, furs and damask and even on buttons and swords. Yet, on the 14th January 1512, a certification was made by Henry VIII to the King's Great Wardrobe to deliver to Blanke a gown of violet cloth, a bonnet and a hat, as a gift for his marriage. Interesting, because Henry VIII and the rest of the royal family were the only ones who were permitted to wear certain rich colours.

The image of Blanke in art history produces an aesthetic and experiential space of possibility and fixed ideas of the history of Britain. The fragments of historic tapestry open a space of experience towards transformations of knowledge, history and experience of race, self, and community.

Serena Lee

I imagined John Blanke as anything I wanted him to be. I suspect he needed to be (and was) 'twice as good' as his fellow trumpeters, doing the same job and not afraid to say it. This would explain what must have been seen as sheer audacity if not impudence to approach the King for greater wages.

Just over 500 years later we are re-imagining him from our contemporary perspective.

For me he foreshadows the coolness of jazz trumpeters half a millennium later; he is sharp (excuse the pun) and always, always aware of what may be coming around the corner.

Dave Lewis
Photographer

David Lewis (2017) *John Blanke*,
210 × 285 mm, digital photographic print
© David Lewis

I imagined John Blanke as a man who was proud and confident in his profession, judging by the way he was able to negotiate a higher wage for himself, and the fact his wife received a gift from the king upon their marriage. I tried to depict Blanke just before an important event, calmly waiting for when his skills were needed.

Joe Lillington
Illustrator

Joe Lillington (2015) *John Blanke*, 201 × 290 mm, pencil on paper

'[John Blanke] is what would now be called of a different race but then was seen as being of a different skin colour'

Professor Kate Lowe
Professor of Renaissance History and Culture, and Co-director of the
Centre for Renaissance and Early Modern Studies (CREMS)

John Blanke and Acceptance of Difference

John Blanke's double inclusion on the Westminster Tournament Roll of 1511 invites a riff on the intriguing issue of changing attitudes to difference. It shows that there is no straight line over time leading from non-acceptance to acceptance of difference; the present is not necessarily more accepting of difference than various other periods in the past.

The most striking and interesting aspect of the portrayal for me is how John Blanke is depicted wearing a multicoloured hat or 'turban'. Not only is his skin colour different to that of his 'white' colleagues – a difference about which no choice could have been made either by him or by others – but in addition a major form of difference that is of his own choosing – his head-gear – also sets him apart from his fellow trumpeters. Many layers of behaviour and attitude are revealed by this representation.

He is what would now be called of a different race but then was seen as being of a different skin colour. He has chosen to wear (insisted on wearing?) a head covering instead of being bare-headed, he has been officially sanctioned to do this not in the private sphere but as a salaried member of a royal corps processing publicly at Westminster, the seat of English monarchical power, in celebration of the birth of the heir to the throne, and to top it all the image of him wearing this major marker of difference was recorded twice at the time, and has survived for 500 years.

The multicoloured (brown and yellow/green and gold) patterned cloth of the head-gear is a religious and cultural, rather than a fashion, statement, and must signal that John Blanke was a Muslim, or at least had been raised in a Muslim cultural context.

In the roll the head-gear is not shown as a piece of folded and twisted cloth (which is what a turban is) but as a hat; that is, the illuminator seems to have focused on the decorative traits of colour and pattern instead of representing how the cloth was wound around the head. This prioritising is in line with the function of the roll as an heraldic record of an event, where an accurate representation of style takes second place to an accurate representation of heraldic features.

The roll allows us to glimpse an occasion on which the Tudor court permitted one of its employees to wear a marker of Islamic religious and cultural difference that contravened the normal insistence on the homogeneity of livery in quite an extraordinary fashion.

Professor Kate Lowe

'I chose to feature [John Blanke] consciously using his evidence as a way of developing my students' historical skills'

Dan Lyndon
Lead Practitioner for Humanities, Park View School
Fellow of the Schools History Project

John Blanke was my Gateway Drug to Black British History

Having studied African history at university and as a history teacher in a school in West London in the early 1990s, I was very keen to increase the diversity of the curriculum that my students were studying. With the honourable exception of Hakim Adi's book on Black British history, school textbooks were exclusively focusing on the slave trade and the American civil rights movement. I wanted my students to study individuals and events that connected to them and so I started to search out for Black British stories that could be woven into the mainstream KS3 curriculum.

When it came to teaching Tudor history, I delved into my copy of *Staying Power* by Peter Fryer and came across the description of John Blanke and his role in the Tudor courts. I was mesmerised. A quick google search led me to the iconic image of Blanke from the Westminster Roll and I immediately had my hook for the lesson.

- Who is this guy?
- What is he doing here?
- What else do we know about him?
- What does his presence tell us about other Africans in Britain at the time?

Once the image had piqued the students' interest then we could delve a bit deeper into Black presence in Tudor times. I came across Miranda Kaufmann's research on Elizabeth I and her proclamations about the Blackmoores and built the second part of the lesson around that fascinating story. John Blanke always stayed with me and when I was choosing source materials for a baseline test for my year 7s I chose to feature him consciously using his evidence as a way of developing my students' historical skills.

A few years later I was invited to write what was to become a seminal article for *Teaching History* about teaching multicultural British history and I used John Blanke as an example of how we can drip-feed Black history into the mainstream curriculum. And moving forward to the present day when I co-write a textbook on the history of migration to Britain, John Blanke opens the chapter on the early modern period.

Thank you John, for helping me take my first steps on this amazing journey of discovery. I hope I have done you proud.

Dan Lyndon

For sources see page 259

I imagined John Blanke as physically and emotionally strong but occasionally lonely, especially when neither playing music nor working. Perhaps before his marriage? Because this feeling is quite universal I have tried to make this image timeless. I have used a fleur-de-lys pattern in the window screens to signify commonalities in Moorish, medieval, royal and modern design.

Seema Manchanda
Artist

Seema Manchanda (2017) *John Blanke*, 210 × 297 mm, pencil on paper

I imagined John Blanke as a lone black person in the white context of the Royal Court, with all that implies. I feel he was a proud and confident man, an accomplished trumpeter, who felt sufficiently secure in his musical expertise and thus his position at the court of Henry VIII, to request a pay rise. This could be the first recorded demand for equal pay!

Janet Manning
Artist

Janet Manning (2017) *John Blanke*, 210 × 290 mm, quilted art and mixed-media textile

'Were Juan de Salonia, [trumpeter to Prince John of Spain] and John Blanke the same trumpeter?'

Dr Emma Luisa Cahill Marrón
International Outreach Coordinator – Art, Power, and Gender Research Group

Were Juan de Salonia and John Blanke the same trumpeter?

From 1493 until his death on October 1497, Prince John of Spain, heir to King Ferdinand of Aragon and Queen Isabella of Castile and brother to Catherine of Aragon, employed a trumpeter named Juan de Salonia. He was part of a group of six musicians playing this instrument in his household. The first two to join his service, Juan de Cieza and Alonso de Valdenebro, started in 1492. The other three were Juan de Cuadros, Francisco de Medina, and Fernando de Aguilera. The only other time Salonia is mentioned in these records was in June 1501 when a certain master Colin received a reward in Granada 'because the Turks from the isles of Thesalonia cut his arm in the service of the king and queen'.

In Strabo's *Geography*, Salonia was in the Roman province of Bithynia, a land that covers today's northwest Turkey. In 1325 it was conquered by the Ottoman Empire becoming the Bolu Providence. The Ottoman Empire included a diverse range of ethnic groups across the territories it controlled not just Southeast Europe and Western Asia, but also North Africa so Juan de Salonia could well have been Black.

Juan de Salonia seems to be the only trumpeter with a foreign origin in Prince John's service. After his master's death, he is not mentioned in the royal accounts again. Could this mean that Juan de Salonia and the other five trumpeters started serving someone else? When Catherine of Aragon travelled to England in 1501, the source mentions six trumpeters, but their names are not included. In one of Queen Isabella's extraordinary payments in February 1502, these six trumpeters' wages are cited.

In May 1503 one of Prince John's former trumpeters, Alonso de Valdenebro, is mentioned in the Spanish queen's financial records receiving a reward for some damages that he suffered travelling to England to serve the Princess of Wales. Could this mean that Juan de Salonia was, along with Alonso de Valdenebro, amongst the musicians that travelled with the Princess of Wales in 1501?

Can you imagine that, in reality, Juan de Salonia and John Blanke are the same trumpeter?

Dr Emma Luisa Cahill Marrón

'[John Blanke's] tiny image – tiny, but invaluable as both portrait and history'

Jan Marsh
Historian and Curator

An Invaluable Tudor Portrait

Portraits of non-noble sitters in Tudor Britain are very rare, because this new form of visual art in the 16th century was aimed at sustaining the fame and power of high-status individuals. Lesser folk might have pictorial images in woodcuts or manuscript illustrations, but these were often crude and typically generic representations, not recognisable figures. The Black trumpeter in the 1511 Tournament Roll is therefore amazing on many levels.

As the earliest depiction of an individual of African ancestry in British pictorial culture it demonstrates how in recognition of his unique or at least special qualities he literally stood out from his fellow trumpeters, shown as a team of lookalikes in the yellow and grey livery worn by all attendants in the procession. They are bareheaded, too, whereas he wears a turban, which indicates the personal appearance of a known individual, just like the dark skin carefully delineated alongside dozens of white-faced figures. As it happens, the Roll's illuminator forgot to colour in his visible right hand holding the trumpet, which remains as pale as the others'.

This is more of a 'thumbnail' image than a carefully observed portrait in the classic manner exemplified by Holbein's drawings of Tudor courtiers, but it is a likeness which contemporaries would recognise, of a known figure in the musical retinue.

Even more remarkably, it has proved possible to name this exceptional musician using Court records. Or at least find the name given to him at the courts of Henries VII and VIII. It's too bad there is no surviving record of his real, or original name, which might have pointed to a country or region of birth. 'John Blanke' has the hallmark of official convenience, although one wonders whether it derives from a functionary entering the name of 'John Black', a common way of registering dark-skinned foreigners, or from 'John -----', a literal blank line in the absence of a familiar cognomen.

One can assume he came as an immigrant to England, presumably in the entourage of Katherine or Catalina of Aragon when she arrived to marry Arthur Tudor in 1501. Following Arthur's death, she married Henry VIII in 1509, and the Westminster Tournament was held to mark the birth of their son, who sadly died within six weeks. Katherine's later life was no happier, but John Blanke evidently throve as a court musician, and may well have had numerous British descendants.

Tudor portraiture also flourished, on a rather grander scale than this tiny image – tiny, but invaluable as both portrait and history.

Jan Marsh

For sources see page 259

I imagined John Blanke as a compelling man who used his musical talent, charm and position in the royal courts to shout out to the world that 'I am here'.

Maya Martin
Artist

Maya Martin (2023) *John Blanke*, 210 × 297 mm, ink on card

'[John Blanke, a] blank slate onto which we project our duelling notions of blackness and Britishness'

S. I. Martin
Author, Researcher, Journalist

The Blanke Slate

We see him depicted at the Westminster Tournament Roll from 1511, the sole non-white face amongst a row of mounted trumpeters. His colleagues stare intently ahead, appearing to focus on their work. John blows his trumpet with his eyes flicked upwards perhaps in an expression of exasperation or maybe with boredom at never being able to escape his role as the King's 'blacke trumpete'. He alone wears a turban in contrast to the other trumpeters whose hair is unbound. John can never be anonymous.

The little we know of what lies behind his strange expression deepens the mystery and seems to have set us a host of historical problems we've yet to resolve.

His origins are unknown. We don't know if he came from west or north Africa. Did he arrive in the entourage of Catherine of Aragon in 1501 or that of another noble from the Iberian Peninsula, or was he an independent traveller? Had he previously been employed in a court in northern Europe where the practice of having Africans as walking, talking objets d'art had been long in fashion? Perhaps he may have ventured down from Scotland where the presence of Moorish taubronars (drummers) was also a feature.

Thereafter cliches abound. The details of John Blanke's life seem to set a template for comprehending and interpreting the African presence in Britain for centuries to come.

John's image is the first representation of a historical Black person in Britain. He is both a musician and a servant in an 'elite' household. The figures of the Black entertainer and the black servant (male and female both turbanned) are stock characters in the narrative of Black British history. He is a Black man who not only marries a white English woman in 1512 but does so with King Henry VIII's apparent blessing and a gift of a *'gown of violet cloth'* and a bonnet.

Did John Blanke belong to a specialist cavalry unit as has been suggested? If so, then he can be safely placed at the beginning of a tradition of turbanned and befezzed Africans who would man British army regiments into the 20th century.

But he is not enslaved. Here John Blanke steps from the shadow of stereotype. He was paid 8d (eight pence) per day by both King Henry VII and Henry VIII. Not only was he waged, he also bargained with King Henry VIII for a pay increase, beseeching him as a *'true and faithfull servant'* to grant him pay equivalent to that received by a deceased co-worker. This action makes John the first Black (and successful!) petitioner.

John Blanke remains a mystery, a blank slate onto which we project our duelling notions of blackness and Britishness.

I imagined John Blanke as a real person not fragmented to fit a box or category of inclusiveness; as a king of simple authenticity based on his on life; as a unique individual; a legacy; made connections and embraced the connection he had.

Reminder to me of the many journeys travelled and still to travel.

A bastion of pride and freedom throughout life; a key part of King Henry's creative outpour.

Randolph Matthews
Vocal Performer

The Call of John Blanke

Written and performed by Randolph Matthews

'Representation matters as by seeing ourselves in stories, we learn and dream of what we could become and achieve'

Seema McArdle
Writer, Educator and PunGeordie

John Blanke: Representation Matters

When I began plotting my middle-grade time-slip adventure, I deliberately included characters that I identified with in some way: a British Asian girl, a white working-class boy and Black Tudor trumpeter, John Blanke.

As a schoolteacher, I'd witnessed children of colour respond with joy and curiosity, when we shared books featuring characters with whom they identified. Yet, as a child, all the books I'd read were written by white authors, with only white characters. Even when I studied Tudor England in my history 'A' level and degree, Black Tudors weren't mentioned.

So, in 2021, I did an internet search, asking, 'Were there any Black Tudors?' and John Blanke appeared!

I've been inspired by John Blanke and imagine him as…

Cool, proud and resilient: From being enslaved to becoming a Royal Trumpeter who commanded respect.

Strong and fit: Mentally strong to have endured and achieved so much against the odds and physically fit to have sat on a horse for hours, whilst playing his trumpet without falling off!

Highly talented and valued: Why else would he feature twice on an important scroll, be gifted a purple velvet cap and gown from the king and receive the huge wage increase he'd requested? Henry VIII loved music (he even wrote some) so perhaps John had jamming sessions with the king.

Representation matters as by seeing ourselves in stories, we learn and dream of what we could become and achieve. To know that Black people existed in Britain in the past is powerful as it counteracts the racist rhetoric we hear in society claiming people of colour are 'foreigners' that don't belong.

We may never find a better representation of a Black Tudor than John Blanke and this is why I believe in celebrating his amazing journey, talents and phenomenal success.

Seema McArdle

I imagined John Blanke as a musician, then as now with a clear sense of his own worth, and a likely background at court in southern Europe. Henry VIII a highly respected musician and composer. I was intrigued by the meeting of two worlds and imagined mutual respect.

Pete McCaldon
Artist

Peter McCaldon (2017) *John Blanke*, 210 × 290 mm, white chalk on black card

I Imagined John Blanke as being from a wealthy family somewhere like modern day Mali. In his lifetime it would have been a very wealthy nation. I imagine him to be an accomplished horseman and musician, coming from a culture that valued both.

I imagine that in the court of Henry VII he would have been liked and respected for his skills and background.

In my picture he is talking with Christopher Urswick who was another employee of the court. They are discussing Erasmus and joking about how bad he is with horses.

Alex McKenzie
Artist

Alex McKenzie (2021) *John Blanke Meets Christopher Urswick*, 195 × 295 mm, ink on paper

I imagined John Blanke as a complex man full of character and emotion, who wrote and performed his own music during the quieter moments, boldly testing the boundaries of his art. The artists of 1511 struggled to capture his depth, and here he also resists my urge to caricature him. I cannot begin this image with black and white. In order to try and understand John Blanke, I need burnt umber and African gold.

Pen Mendonça
Graphic Facilitator and Cartoonist

Pen Mendonça (2018) *John Blanke*, 210 × 297 mm, digital print

I imagined John Blanke as smiling as he rubs Argan Oil into his arms and sees the mahogany reflected in the melanin of his muscled limbs as he walks through the court of the 'Petulant King'.

I picture him as one of my ancestors who have come and gone unheralded, mythical beings who have been handed down through the generations until they are now grainy pictures in the mind.

The ancestors of the slavery years haunt me with a melancholy that comes from knowing that no matter what potential they had as they travelled the nine months from conception to the birth canal, most of it would not be realised. The notion that a human being still attached to the umbilical cord of its mother is a slave is the most unbearable of things. Before that child is born, before it takes the first suck of its mother's teat, even before its conception, the potential of that child is enslaved. Imagine if that was your child.

I am a descendant of slaves and the result of slavery. The Atlantic trade was the starting point in a new and perilous journey that nature made in my name a few hundred years ago. I am in the middle of that journey and the final destination is unknown.

Those realities that have made me also denied who I ought to have been from ever becoming real. That drifted me off into a parallel universe where, hopefully, I grew up in the love, security and traditions of the past thousands of years in the river beds, plains and valleys of West Africa.

The new me after all this time will look you in the eye and proudly say, I was, I am and I will become again what I was always intended to be. I give great homage to my ancestors.

I imagine John Blanke, still smiling, as he reads this and realises that he was one of the lucky ones. He avoided the Maafa, The Great Maangamizi.

Roy Merchant
(1949-2022)
Poet and Storyteller

Seeking Mr Blanke
by Roy Merchant

I never got to know you, Mr Blanke,
We travelled in two different slipstreams of time.
Your journey was at the start of the Maafa,
The Great Maangamizi.
And I followed in its aftermath.

Why has your presence stayed blank Mr Blanke?
Faded from history like a footprint in the sand and rain.
Just a few tantalising images,
And an enigmatic name,
To remind us that you once graced us
With your essence, soul, energy and life.

But, who were you really Mr Blanke?
I mean, I saw you at the back, amongst the crowd of musicians.
A black trumpeter sitting on a horse.
Standing out like a beautiful ebony masterpiece,
In a white marbled hall.
Did you feel precious or forlorn?
Nauseous or proud in your solitude?
My empathic disposition, makes me think that you felt out of place,

Alone, All alone.

Seeking solace in a barren, foreign land.

Did your talent drive you into the courts of the Catholic Kings?
Was it from Spain to England you came?
Playing trumpets for the First and Second Tudor Kings,
Wasting time, playing simple specious things.
When a concerto was running around your mind.

Where did you come from Mr Blanke?
What Fields, Oceans, Deserts had you travelled?
To end up playing the trumpet,
In the court of the usurper of thrones,
And then his petulant son.

We know you were not a Blackamoor Vassal,
Or a simple Muslim Thrall.
But, were you a captured warrior?
Forced to degrade and denigrate himself.

Did you look at them all and smile?
At their lack of intellect.
To you, brought up in the traditions of Alhambra,
They would seem to know nothing of art,
Nothing of literature,
Nothing about nothing it seemed.

Maybe you were a victim of the Reconquista,
When the Catholic Kings replaced the Moors.
Did your world come to an end in 1492?
In Alhambra's Patio Arrayanes,
Or was it at El Patio Mexuar,
That King Ferdinand took control of your life?

Did you know Catalina de Montril?
Katherine Of Aragon's chambermaid.
Were you, like her, a captured Moor?
Was being exiled from Al-Andalus the price you both paid,
For staying loyal too long to your Moorish King?
Did you and Catalina become lovers, before she returned to Spain?
Was pure friendship the bond of your choice?
Or, was she just someone you heard about?
The retinue being so vast.

We know you were wed in the first month of Fifteen-Twelve,
We wish we could have seen Mrs Blanke.
Was she too, of dark melanin?
Or was she of a lighter hue?

I can imagine you in your violet robe and hat,
Your wife in the bonnet from the king.
At last, you had found some happiness,
And your travailing travel could come to an end.

We do not hear much more from you,
From Fifteen-Thirteen you were gone from view.
Did you go back to Italy, Spain or France?
Or become invisible in survival's dance?

And as I sit here gazing at your image,
I muse and say;
"So, who were you, Mr Blanke?
Sitting there on your liveried horse,
Proudly playing like you have never played before.
Keeping your thoughts deeply hidden,
In the dark, deep, propitious recesses,
Of your beautiful melanin soul."

© Roy Merchant 2018

'In January 1512 Henry VIII instructed the Great Wardrobe to provide clothes to "John Blak (sic), our trompeter," as a wedding present from himself'

Ninya Mikhaila
Historical Costumier

What Did John Blanke's Wedding Clothes Look Like?

In January 1512 Henry VIII instructed the Great Wardrobe to provide clothes to 'John Blak (sic), our trompeter,' as a wedding present from himself. The garments are described as 'a gown of violet cloth, &c., including a bonnet and a hat'. A further document at The British Library, discovered by Sean Cunningham (see page 72), details the payments made to the suppliers of the materials, and to the tailor for making the garments.

Transcription of tailoring account for John Blanke's wedding outfit:

> by warrant dated at Greenwich, 14 January in the this year –1512 – for John Blak (sic)
>
> Richard Smith for iiij yards velvet cloth for a gown at vj s viij d the yard — xxvi s viij d
> Edward Goodwyn for 98 skins of blac spanysh bogie to furre the same at xij d — iiij li xviij s
> William Hylton for making of the same gown — vij d
> Edward Goodwyn for furring of the same gown — iiij s vi d
> Fraunces Paunsaunt for iij yards blac violet for a doublet at xj a vj d — xxxiij s vj d
> Lewes Harpisfeld for iij yards j qtr white fustian to line the same at viij d — ij s ij d
> John Harvill for a yard canvas to line the same — iij d
> William Hilton for making of the same doublet — iiij s
> Richard Smyth for a pair of scarlet hose — viij s
> Robert Hynd for a bonet price — ij s
> Item a hatt, price xix d
> Summa ix li xxiij nova emptcione [sum £9 new purchases]

Money notation (pre decimalisation in February 1971) li – pounds (£) s – shillings (20s to the pound) d – pennies (12d to the shilling). The j terminates the Roman numeral entry for example iij is iii or xviij is xviii.

1511-12 accounts of Andrew Windsor, the keeper of the Great Wardrobe, held at the British Library (BL Egerton MS 3025 folio 18r)

This document paints a much fuller picture of John Blanke's wedding outfit. Most of the expense went into the primary, and outermost garment, which was the gown. John's gown was cut from four yards of violet cloth and furred with 98 black lambskins called 'bogie'. The name for the fur derives from Bougie, a medieval Moorish kingdom in North Africa where it was originally imported from. Violet cloth for gowns was given to other royal servants including William Croughton, the king's hosier in 1511 and Richard Mayre, one of the yeomen of the Ewery in 1512. Both of these gowns were also furred with black lambskin, though it is interesting to note that the provision for Richard Mayre was for Irish lambskin, whereas John's Blanke's was to be of the more costly and prestigious Spanish bogie.

John was also provided with a doublet of black velvet, interlined with canvas and lined with white fustian (a linen and cotton mix) as well as a pair of scarlet hose, a bonnet and a hat. Velvet was the most expensive silk fabric and scarlet was a high-quality wool cloth, usually dyed red

An impression of the whole outfit can be seen in Michael Perry's illustration of the garments provided for William Croughton in 1511. William wears his gown over a skirted tawny jacket which partially obscures the black doublet below. The cloth allowed for the gown was half a yard more than John's, and the garment would therefore have been a bit more generously cut in the width of the skirts and sleeves, but the overall appearance of colours and styles is very much how John Blanke would have looked on his wedding day.

Ninya Mikhaila

For sources see page 259

Michael Perry's illustration of the garments provided for William Croughton in 1511

I imagined John Blanke as a musician and storyteller; wearing his charisma, his virtuosity, his new Christianity, his mastery of yet another European language, like a richly-embroidered coat that he can never take off. It protects him from harm, at the cost of masking his true self.

> *I was so homesick there were tears standing in my eyes. But homesick for what? For a feeling of belonging? For freedom to speak my feelings unchecked?*
>
> John Blanke, Act 1, Scene 15
The Trumpet & The King

And yet he triumphs. He is a touchstone.

For me John Blanke is the quintessential immigrant artist, and the immigrant artist walks alone. John shines at the court of two Tudor kings, but if he ever loses the king's favour, like all immigrants there is no family net to break his fall.

Playwrights like risk. There is plenty of risk in John's story of success.

I grew up in Indonesia: a Muslim country, and I'm fascinated by Islam's 800-year rule of Spain. Many scholars believe John came to England from Spain, giving him a breadth of cultural experience that was irresistible to me. That he was a court musician during the early days of Henry VIII's wild, music-mad kingship gave me a context for friendship between these two young men at the intersection between talent and power.

During the writing of *The Trumpet & The King* (2019 – 2022), I realised that I needed a place for John and Henry to meet as equals. The play is set in the afterlife. In limbo they are two souls, trying to reconstruct the details of their youth, and every object they pick up plunges them back to a different memory, often with conflicting results.

I planted a betrayal at the heart of their story, and let it unfold from there.

I have now staged a prototype performance of this two-person play in the summer of 2022: a tour of Northern Ireland followed in 2023. Now I am planning to take the work beyond.

Andrea Montgomery
Playwright and Director

Poster for *The Trumpet & The King* (2019-2022), written & directed by Andrea Montgomery

I imagine John Blanke as a musician, who follows his heart and art where music leads him.

Sheba Montserrat
Performance Poet

The Original Don

Yes, Big Man.
Yes you,
John Blanke.

Ride that horse, And blow that horn!
Not for sheep in the meadow, Or for cows in the barn!
But for us in the future
So we know what a gwaan!

Yes John Blanke.
Yes Dada!
Blowin'
And riding in the Kings Parade
That's, Just how history is made.

Let your horn, proclaim
That nobility came
Before
Forced humility.

And who didn't hear you,
Can see you.
Coz what,
They put you on tapestry
Documentation add to mystery.

Woy!
John.
Big musician man.
The trumpet don!
The Afrikan.....

Superstar!

Drop, trumpet cool
Just like Miles,
With a wonder
Just like Stevie.

And in the words of the Banton,
Walk like champion
Talk like a champion!
John Blanke,
… the original Don!

© Sheba Montserrat 2018

I imagined John Blanke as a very confident, talented musician. He had enough faith in his own talent to demand and receive a pay rise, and he must have had confidence – there's no hiding when you're the lead brass player! But there's also mystery. What was his real name? Is John Blanke a nickname someone gave him? How did he feel about that? Was he ever enslaved? Even if he lived in freedom, he would undoubtedly have faced prejudice. Despite that, he reached the top of his game and I like to think of him enjoying his success.

Kate Morrison
Writer

Fanfare
by Kate Morrison

Enter the trumpets,
Those blowhards; the big-talking, deep-drinking brass players
Who wet their lips with ale before the joust and will wet them again after,
Toasting the new Prince.

Enter John Blanke,
Star musician, a blaze of silver-and-gilt,
Right arm burning with the trumpet's weight,
Left hand light on the reins, keeping the horse in line,
Sweat salting his mouth.

Like life at court, it takes all his strength, skill and balance.
For a king, only the best will do –
"Lucky for me," he thinks, filling his lungs with triumph, "I am."

Fanfare. The notes ring like new-minted gold,
Coin that can't be hoarded, stolen or spent
Flung up to the welkin, the blue sky emblazoned with music.

Watching him, the court artist wishes he could draw
The sound of trumpets; the glitter of it.
Failing that, he'll sketch the man whose gift it is to gilt the air.

Exit John Blanke, into history. Your name is not the one they gave you
But the one your mother whispered in your ear,
That quiet music. Tell her your fame outlasted any man who harmed you.

© Kate Morrison 2022

I imagined John Blanke as an impressive, glamorous, flamboyant and intensely talented presence, in the group context of the collective shine, brilliance and beauty of the King's Royal Trumpeters. This must have been an arresting group of men, clad in costly garments, making glorious music and riding high up on their majestic, gleaming horses. They probably set many hearts racing. The King's Royal Trumpeters were likely the subject of romantic daydreams, the rock stars of their day.

Angeline Morrison
Folk and Traditional Singer, Songwriter and Multi-instrumentalist

The Royal Trumpeter

(Music and lyrics by Angeline Morrison)

John Blanke, John Blanke
High upon a chestnut horse I ride,
All clad in the cloth of gold
With King Henry's Royal Trumpetmen.

In this year of 1511, a son was born unto the Queen and King
Let England rejoice! Westminster shake
With feasting, and with jousting, and with trumpeting.

John Blanke, John Blanke
High upon a chestnut horse I ride,
All clad in the cloth of gold
With King Henry's Royal Trumpetmen.

All the night we polished till our trumpet's gleamed like stars,
Sweet notes resounding to announce the King Henry,
And to my heart's delight,
My wage was doubled, for the King was pleased with me.

John Blanke, John Blanke
High upon a chestnut horse I ride,
All clad in the cloth of gold
With King Henry's Royal Trumpetmen.

To be a Royal Trumpeter takes skills so rare,
To serve the King with horsemanship and music fine.
O, then it's to make merrie with my comrades bold!
What life could be so venturesome and sweet as mine?

Chorus

The Royal Trumpeter

Angeline Morrison

'Not only does [John Blanke] appear on entry with the rest of the King's musicians, he also appears on exit, therefore the only identifiable person (other than the King) to appear twice on the roll'

Avril Nanton
Director, Avril's Walks and Talks

A Tour Guide's View To John Blanke

Tour guides who work around London need to know everything about everything. All over London there is history that is revealed to the tourist as they walk around with their guide. The guide stops at each stop and points out something which has a history to it and which they hope the tourists will find interesting.

Imagine then what you would point out to someone who is on a tour with you about John Blanke. John Blanke has been part of London's history since around the 1500s – but how many people have heard of him? Who was he? What did he do to become famous? Why is a tour guide talking about him?

The 1511 Westminster Tournament Roll is a roll that records the joust called by Henry VIII in February 1511 to celebrate the birth of his son with Catherine of Aragon. Although Henry is the undisputed central figure, the figure that has come to the fore nowadays is that of John Blanke, Henry's black trumpeter.

Not only does he appear on entry with the rest of the King's musicians, he also appears on exit, therefore the only identifiable person (other than the King) to appear twice on the roll. Although the roll is dedicated to the King, his double appearance on the roll ensures that he stands out from the crowd. The other reason he stands out is he is the only musician wearing a turban of sorts. He's clearly styled his turban to what suits him and feels comfortable wearing it. He's a man who likes to be different. Whether he likes it or not he stands out purely based on the colour of his skin – which he knows. He is wearing the same uniform as the others therefore it is clear that he isn't just someone who has stumbled upon this event and joined in. He's also carrying the King's standard. In effect he's 'one of them'. He fits in with everyone else, he's doing what everyone else is doing i.e. celebrating the birth of the King's son. He's not different; he's the same. His needs and wants are the same as everyone else.

In effect, John Blanke has become famous just because he was black. Famous for being black wouldn't become popular until some time later – so he was way ahead of his time without realising it!

Tour guides will need to do their research about this amazing character who lived in London at a time when it was thought there were no Black people in London, and those that were here were slaves, yet here we find one in the King's court. How would that go down with the UKIP voter of today I wonder?

Avril Nanton

I imagined John Blanke as a man with great discipline, commitment and absolute professionalism – he had to have these qualities in order to be chosen to play for the King. He was an elite cavalry trumpeter, the training is extensive and arduous, the hours are long. It was incredibly humbling to be asked to be the modern-day trumpeter in memory of John Blanke (JB). As a black trumpeter in the British Army, I appreciate how big an achievement it was for JB to be accepted and given the opportunity to serve in the royal courts. Even today, it is challenging to become a musician in the Household Cavalry.

Lawrence Narhkom
Lance Sergeant
Army Musician

Project Director's note
Lawrence's trumpeting announced the opening and closing of John Blanke Live! Symposia at The College of Arms and the National Trust's Sutton House. Both times his playing attracted many compliments and greatly added to the evenings' success.

© Photograph Michael Ohajuru
Lance Sergeant Lawrence Narhkom
Royal Corps of Army Musicians (2017)

I imagined John Blanke as someone with not only talent but a deep adoration for the instrument. I imagine him to be a force to be around, so much so that he caught the King's attention and became one of his trumpeters.

Jess Nash
Illustrator

Jess Nash (2023) *John Blanke*, 210 × 297 mm, ink on paper

I Imagine John Blanke as musing on the happenings in his life which have brought him to his position at the court of the mercurial Henry the Eighth. I imagine him remembering that it was his musical skills which have given him acceptance and recognition. Now the pageantry, colour and ceremonial are part of his life. But he also ponders on the future. Will he return to his place of birth? Will he be able to tell his story to his grandchildren? Will it all last?

Elaine Nason
Print Maker and Painter

I imagined John Blanke as a bold and brassy leader of social change, using his position, instrument and talents to bring about freedom, humanity, dignity, harmony, civil rights and social justice.

Dave Neita
Lawyer and Poet

Tribute To John Blanke
By David Neita

The music you made as on the horseback you sat playing the royal bold brass instrument
Lions from African adorn the banner with horn held aloft, and you bedecked resplendent
You cut a majestic poise
Your music cut through the noise
The scene is one of elation
But your eyes – deep desolation

Your people dispossessed, tortured and bruised!
Could you hear Miles Davis' kind of blues?
Paul Dunbar's caged bird with its pain so keen?
Louis Armstrong's nobody knows the trouble I've seen?
Dizzy Gillespie, Hugh Masekela, Dean Fraser, Charlie Parker? Civil Rights Movement,
 Human Rights, Black Lives Matter!
John Blanke, we can still hear the music you played all those centuries ago
Your symphony still stirs our souls today as we fight for a better tomorrow

© David Neita 2016

I imagined John Blanke as a figure of intrigue and prominence when I first encountered him depicted as one of the Royal Trumpeters in the Westminster Tournament Roll. This artwork highlighted his unique position through the Royal Tudor coat of arms adorning each trumpet, marking a significant court event where John stood out prominently.

My fascination grew as he was the only Black person featured, sparking questions about his origins and his life at the pinnacle of English society during the 15th and 16th centuries.

I pondered over how John acquired his musicianship and adapted to the customs of the Royal English court. Was he perhaps part of a royal court in his homeland before being presented to England's court? What kind of man was he, and how did he interact with his peers? Was his living arrangement among the court's staff in a dormitory, or did he have a family and a home of his own?

The source material I had been given on John Blanke was not enough – it answered too few of these questions for me to create an image. So I decided to imagine my own source to answer my questions. I imagined I had discovered the works of a distinguished academic who had delved into the history of 15th and 16th century literature. Their research revealed insights from a Book of Hours owned by a lady of the Tudor court, who was the young widow of a lord linked to Henry's court. In her notes, she describes her interactions with John Blanke, 'a musician of great skill'. She details their conversations about religion, philosophy, astrology, astronomy, and their mutual appreciation for nature, discussing the wildlife and natural environments of their respective countries.

Through her writings, I glimpsed the depth of John's knowledge and his ability to engage in profound discussions on various subjects, revealing his well-rounded intellect and curiosity. These notes provided a rare, personal insight for me into John Blanke's life, allowing me to reimagine this enigmatic man who navigated his role within the complexities of the English Tudor court.

Ormond Noonan
Artist

Ormond Noonan (2013) *John Blanke*, 225 × 300 mm, watercolour on paper

'The archive presents John Blanke thinly, as a sketch, but still a necessary opening for us in the present'

Dr Temi Odumosu
Assistant Professor and Curator at the University of Washington Information School

Marked

In tints of black and ashen brown
Translucent fading dyes
Emerald-capped
Rare
Costume livened by gold
With emblems in bloody crimson and vibrant azure
Aged gracefully as rolling sky or sea
Mounted on horseback
In lined procession
For ritual
Mouth on trumpet like Dizzy Gillespie's twin
Mid-breath
(Somewhere there is an echo for that sound)
Sparse cursive words
Mundane
Elegant
Cite remuneration for true and faithful service to a king
And thus in small lasting marks
You make your presence known
A question, yes
But a satisfying mystery

John Blanke was here. That is a fact. This African man in Tudor England left traces behind. We might imagine him treading footprints on soil. And then, intimately, like all of us, shed his sweat, dust, blood and skin in the sinews of London streets, on duty at court, and in perpetuity deep within an unmarked grave. But we encounter him first as a material memory. A bodily presence evoked on crinkled paper in paint and ink. Handmade and whispering down the ages. Such are the peculiar consequences of royal attention.

There is much we do not know: his genealogy and kinship ties, a country of origin, and migration story. In short the entire arc of a human saga. Not to mention the substance of his inner life. Hopes, ambitions, sadness, fears. Yes, boldly he petitioned an inadequate wage, but who loved him and whom did he love? Was that the name he was born with? How did he feel about life, as a singular Black man, in an English court?

The archive presents John Blanke thinly, as a sketch, but still a necessary opening for us in the present. His face and words a surrogate for the lost ones. Those other souls (and their network of memories) denied the recognition that comes from acts of mark making. The name Blanke is a loaded irony. For he is the lacuna, and fills it by the same means. This is the bittersweet paradox of the Black subject in Western history and its art. To be seen and not be, concurrently.

How then do we honour the substance of a man's entire life when there is so much we cannot really know? Sweetly, and with care and attention paid also to the silence.

I imagined John Blanke as an unknown figure of history, someone who was probably involved in historic events but not acknowledged. Being a Moor in 16th century England couldn't have been easy. It must have required him to be resilient, diplomatic and focused.

Valentine Ogunba
Rapper and Educator

Forever Moor: John Blanke Rap

Written and performed by Valentine Ogunba

Chorus

Trumpet man blowin' horn while battling scorn,
Go wrong, go right yeah the mind is torn,
In a land so far from where my line was born,
Never doubt I will be forever Moor,
I stand blown' horn while battling scorn,
Go wrong, go right yeah the mind is torn,
In a land so far from where my line was born,
Never doubt I will be forever Moor,

Verse 1

I am he present but unknown,
Skilled of strife I cannot but hold my own,
My horn is me, it and I synonymous,
Unfulfilled so much more than eponymous,
Announced in court as a sounder of the realm,
Many would see me kept back from the helm,
But fate gifts me with the will of a lion,
Warrior Moor sword front aiming side on,
Grief no longer hear now my petition,
Steady my hand lest it turn to sedition,
Why this love that ignites and enrages,
Never wise to unravel a man in stages,
Hold back grief so sire can find rest,
Eye be strong let me see out this test,
Woe my foe until the day that I free her,
Do you not hear my heart beat – CA – TA – LINA

Chorus

Trumpet man blowin' horn while battling scorn,
Go wrong, go right yeah the mind is torn,
In a land so far from where my line was born,
Never doubt I will be forever Moor,
I stand blown' horn while battling scorn,
Go wrong, go right yeah the mind is torn,
In a land so far from where my line was born,
Never doubt I will be forever Moor,

Verse 2

But I was born of the dust, to it I'll return to,
Quiet your cries courage he heard you,
I wish for death lovely she seems,
Welcome my nightmares run from my dreams,
Scared of success gotta stick close,
No need for 6th sense already ghosts,
See myself walking a path of destruction,
Pray through the pain for introductions,
To a new life, to a new soul,
My friend said don't think reach for your goals,
Let the world see a man free of regret,
With all my flaws me I accept,
Blessed to put my conscious to a new sound,
A lifetime speaks spirit profound,
The heavens have seen my story conclude,
But this chapter falls to me to see through,

Chorus

Trumpet man blowin' horn while battling scorn,
Go wrong, go right yeah the mind is torn,
In a land so far from where my line was born,
Never doubt I will be forever Moor,
I stand blowin' horn while battling scorn,
Go wrong, go right yeah the mind is torn,
In a land so far from where my line was born,
Never doubt I will be forever Moor

© 2017 Valentine Ogunba

'[John Blanke] defined by [his] race and ... occupation "the blacke trumpet"'

Adèle Oliver
Writer, Artist, Researcher

John Blanke: Brass in the Belly of the Beast

Warmed by the kiss of taut lips; animated by ancestral secrets held in puffed cheeks; pushed to its limits by determined tongues, the trumpet is one of Black history's most reliable conduits. Through warnings, jubilation, decrees, and celebration, from royal regalia in Buganda, to mediaeval courts in Tudor Britain, plantations across Caribbean, second lines in New Orleans, and carnivals in Brazil, the trumpet has been trusted with our most intimate tales, by our most innovative minds.

John Blanke and his immortalised image – one hand on steed, eyes gazing up towards the sky, head covered in a turban, cheeks stretched thin – is an important part of this lineage.

Dear John,

We know that your trumpet was an instrument of the British institution – a work tool. And work you did. Every day. A record of the first payment to you says as much. In it, you are defined by your race and your occupation 'the blacke trumpet'. A few decades after our last record of you, Henry VIII scratched a burgeoning imperial itch in the Boulonnais, developing an exclusively ethnically English colony there. In the centuries to follow, those who bore the likeness of John Blanke, on British plantations across the New World, would be listed by name, sex, race, occupation. Would any of them be black trumpets too?

John, what did you speak through your trumpet's tantara? Which whispered wants vibrated in its chambers? Which memories were welded to the metal? Which secrets swelled in your sighs? Did you ever trust the brass with your real name?

This, of course, we will never know. What we do know is that our brass-tinged history, across the diaspora, has echoed for longer than we may have thought. Those stories still whistle through our streets. We'll listen out for yours, John

Adèle Oliver

'The King of England thought of himself as close to God. And God was accompanied by trumpets, the King needed his own trumpets and John Blanke was one of them'

Onyeka
Author of *Blackamoores: Africans in Tudor England*

Understanding the Context of John Blanke

When I blow with a trumpet, I and all that are with me, then blow ye the trumpets also on every side of all the camp, and say, The sword of the LORD, and of Gideon.

Judges 7:17, King James Version of the Bible, 1611.

This passage from the Bible illustrates why the trumpet and its sound, neigh its power revealed in sound, was so important to people in early modern England. Blanke was a man of African descent, a trumpeter who lived in England in the 16th century. His name Blanke may have been a misspelling that stuck of blacke. Indeed he is often referred to in official records simply as the black trumpeter. Blanke's name could also be a joke or a pun of the French word blanc meaning white. But his profession was not a joke. He was not part of a sideshow, but the central arc that made the Westminster celebrations sacred and important. He appears twice on the Roll created in 1511 to commemorate the celebrations for the birth of the son of Katherine of Aragon and Henry VIII. Blanke may have originated from the Iberian Peninsula where people of African descent in the 16th century represented a significant part of that population. Black trumpeters were important and popular throughout 16th century Europe. They were some of the most well-respected musicians and their trumpets were often seen as having the same role as Gideon or Joshua in the Bible. Joshua used his trumpets to knock down the walls of Jericho, his trumpets were magical:

And it shall come to pass, that when they make a long [blast] with the ram's horn, [and] when ye hear the sound of the trumpet, all the people shall shout with a great shout; and the wall of the city shall fall down flat, and the people shall ascend up every man straight before him.

Joshua 6:5

So the people shouted when [the priests] blew with the trumpets: and it came to pass, when the people heard the sound of the trumpet, and the people shouted with a great shout, that the wall fell down flat, so that the people went up into the city, every man straight before him, and they took the city

Joshua 6:20.

It is not surprising that John Blanke was an integral element in another great shout or *L'hostel* that began the Westminster celebrations in 1511. *L'hostel* was not used to knock down the walls of Jericho but to announce to the world that the King of England had a son. The King of England thought of himself as close to God. And God was accompanied by trumpets, the King needed his own trumpets and John Blanke was one of them. What else do we know about this Blanke? We know he petitioned and won a pay increase for his role as a trumpeter, on more than one occasion. His mother was also present in Tudor England and he got married probably on English soil and was issued with a purple gown and a new bonnet. The bonnet was probably similar to the turbans he is wearing in the Tournament Roll. The turban became the ethnic chic for soldiers of African descent in certain British regiments in the 18th century. John Blanke was the Courtney Pine of his time. But so much more, it is not remarkable to have someone now such as him, as the greatest trumpeter in the country or even the world. And it may not have been in 16th century Europe if the images don't lie. But many historians still cry foul! As they reject a plain reading of the image for a historiography situated in modernity. This is more to do with our engrafted modern racial notions than with England's past.

However be careful of superstardom. By making John Blanke an exception we marginalise and make strange his existence. Exceptionalism can help us keep our prejudices. We can marginalise the anomaly. We can say oh John Blanke he was only one man. One man does not maketh an African presence. Why this is political correctness gone mad! But such suppositions are wrong on all accounts. True he is one of the few Africans in the 16th century for whom we have an image that complements written records. But that does not mean Blanke is the only person of African descent in Tudor England. In fact there are other African people in Tudor society who we know far more about. Some of these people may have had a greater impact on that society than Blanke did. But as we are now asked to gild the lily we can say Blanke remains the most recognisable of a rarely depicted population.

Blanke is important and we are celebrating him here. But only when he becomes less important will we actually begin to understand him, England's history, and the African in it more clearly.

John Blanke (or his notoriety?) means there is much more work for us to do.

Onyeka

'Defined as an African ... John Blanke was also an Afro-European ... Blanke's story is both a British and a European story'

Professor Olivette Otele
Distinguished Research Professor of the Legacies and Memory of Slavery, SOAS

John Blanke, an Afro-European

John Blanke, a musician and an entertainer who was also socially engaged in the struggle for equality in wages has challenged our perception of Tudor England. In many ways it could be argued that it is very difficult for us to fully grasp what life was like for Blanke: a young man of African descent trying to make a living in an environment where life was already difficult for the humblest part of the population.

Probably perceived as the exotic 'Other', Blanke had skills that were deemed valuable enough to be around the wealthiest people in the kingdom. He appeared to have carved a place in Tudor society. His role as a petitioner and records about his marriage are testimony to the impact he had on social actors. Defined as an African or a Blackamoore, John Blanke was also an Afro-European. I'm arguing that Blanke's story is both a British and a European story.

His experience is part of the long and fascinating stories of people of African descent. These stories of multiple trajectories tell us about human connections and resilience. Young John Blanke was by no means the only man of African descent who made a place in European society in the 16th century. I am inviting you to consider his story as a chapter in a book that was not available for centuries. Had he lived long enough, Blanke might have reached the prominence of other illustrious Afro-Europeans such as the first Duke of Florence, Alessandro de Medici and Granada born Juan Latino.

John Blanke did however make his mark and survived the constraints of time long enough tell about his presence through records. It is now our role as entrepreneurs of memory to continue to recall his story and celebrate his presence even five centuries after his death.

Professor Olivette Otele

For sources see page 259

I imagined John Blanke as an individual in possession of exceptional talents. Although 'talent' is a problematic notion in the same way that 'gifted' or 'genius' is often seen to be. I can't conceive of any circumstance where an individual like John Blanke could have survived and prospered, with odds so heavily stacked against his likely success, if he were not an exceptional individual. Talent is, in this context, the word that for me encompasses the breadth of skills that he would have needed to acquire and always quickly, while all the time negotiating unfamiliar challenges.

Eugene Palmer
Artist

Eugene Palmer (2016), *John Blanke*, 225 × 300 mm, pencil on paper

I imagined John Blanke as an adventurous musician who has travelled around the world to share his skills, but retains pride in his African heritage. I've chosen to depict him holding two instruments. The gold trumpet he is playing is based on the European-style one he plays in his Tudor-era depictions, whereas the ivory horn he holds in his left hand is a souvenir from his native country and is modelled after various ivory trumpets from ancient Africa.

Brandon Pilcher
Artist, Essayist and Fiction Writer

Brandon Pilcher (2019), *John Blanke*, 225 × 300 mm, digital print

I imagined John Blanke as a time traveller, a temporal, as well as geographical 'advanced guard', stretching Tudor ears with brand new shades and syncopations. He carried the secret formula to a new music, dropped it, but refused to leave it when he moved on. Like Miles in 1957, he signalled the coming of something new, something literally 'Miles Ahead' of the norm. All he left us was a thumbnail sketch, and a submerged sonic time bomb set to explode in the middle of the 20th century.

Keith Piper
Artist, Researcher

Keith Piper (2019) *John Blanke*, 210 × 290 mm, ink on paper

I imagined John Blanke as a strong, talented and unique individual with many stories to tell. My image shows him on a postage stamp, the first of a set of stamps celebrating Influential Black Londoners that I designed for the National Trust at Sutton House in Hackney.

Jane Porter
Illustrator and Author

Jane Porter (2018) *John Blanke stamp*, 210 × 290 mm, digital print

I imagined John Blanke as a cultural bridge – a man of strength and courage who left his homeland in Africa for new adventures up north. I admire him for making a long trek and braving new territories in order to share his musical gift. Blanke bridges the gap between two continents, holding cherished memories and customs from home, and learning different ones in his new country. The colours I chose to represent him in yarn were a medley inspired from the manuscript. His chartreuse turban with gold honours his homeland tradition, while he also adorns the grey and mustard yellow tunic that his fellow trumpeters wear. On this most fitting sparkly yarn, dominant greys and golden yellows represent the interconnection between his new and old homelands, while the red and green specks reflect the memories and sometimes hidden or partially told narratives that add depth and complexity to those of us from the diaspora.

Dr Mary Rambaran-Olm
Medieval Literary Historian and Indie Yarn Dyer

Dr Mary Rambaran-Olm, *John Blanke*, yarn medley crocheted sample 235 × 285 mm a merino wool (woven with sparkle and a bit of nylon)

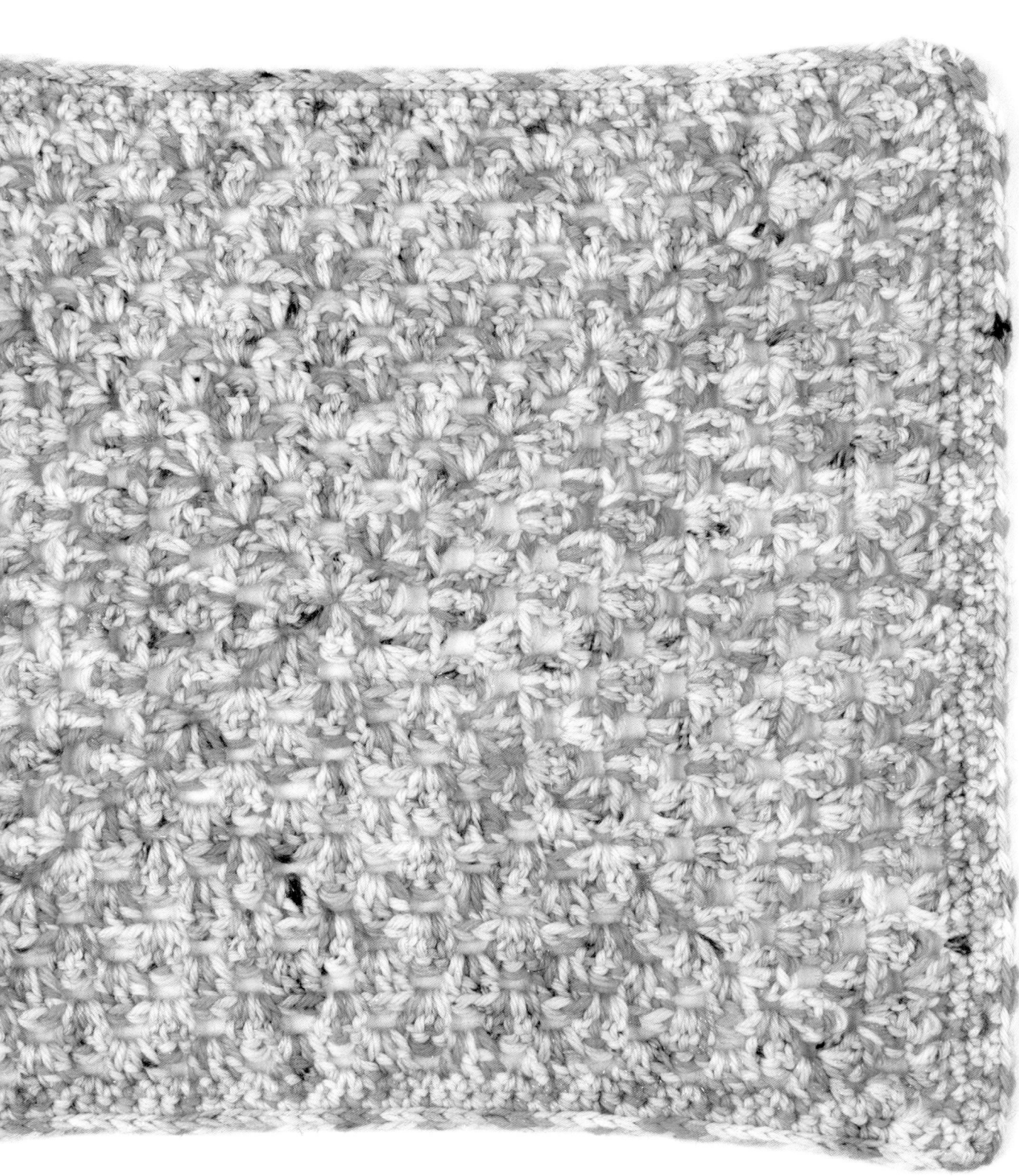

I imagined John Blanke – in creating my artistic interpretation of the late great man I tried to get a feel of the man. In studying the paintings created of him during his life I got a sense that he was a quiet, humble and obviously very talented man. I also felt a sense of sadness and isolation being in a foreign land, far from his own people, culture and customs. These were my thoughts while creating this piece.

Jeremy A Salmon
Illustrator

Jeremy A Salmon(2015) *John Blanke*, 210 × 290 mm, pencil on paper

'So there had been Africans in Britain way before these West Indians arrived!'

Marika Sherwood
(1937-2025)
Writer and Historian

Depiction of a Negro

I attended schools in Australia from 1948, as a Jewish refugee child from Budapest. The only history of Australia we were taught was of the brave British explorers. The focus was on the glories of Britain, with some European history. I did not even know of the existence of Australian Aborigines. For reasons not relevant here, I went to work in Port Moresby, New Guinea when I was 20. That was my introduction to racial discrimination. As someone who had suffered from that in Budapest, I was both furious and heartbroken. Surely, we are all the same, I believed. Of course, I had known nothing about the peoples of New Guinea; even the word 'colony' was unknown to me.

After six months there I returned to Sydney, found a job and went to university as an evening student as I wanted to learn about the world opened to me by my New Guinea experience. I also wanted to learn about the Australian Aborigines. University proved more of a brainwashing experience than an education. But I did get involved in the Aborigines' struggles.

Five years at university; then a job to earn enough money to migrate to the glorious Mother Country in 1965. But it proved to be anything but glorious. There was some social class discrimination in Sydney, but nothing like what I experienced when I began to teach infants/primary schools in Haringey. I was very, very dismayed, shocked. Social class does not influence your ability, your intelligence – all pupils should be treated the same, I believed. (And still believe.)

Even more shocking to me was the racial discrimination. I was asked to teach English to immigrant children in an infants school. I had expected a class of Turkish Cypriots but found in front of me a class of dark-skinned children. All spoke English, but certainly with an accent different from mine and from the Haringey locals. I told the headmistress this. The response was that they were all 'disturbed'. As one of the subjects of my degrees was psychology, this also bewildered me: the children were certainly not 'disturbed'.

I began to ask questions of many people, including the parents coming to pick up their children. So I learned about immigrants from the West Indies, and some West Indian history, and about their experiences of discrimination on arriving in the Mother Country.

I did not even know where the 'West Indies' was! Searched for maps and histories. Very, very few in the local libraries. Certainly nothing about why these families had come to England.

Moving to teach in a comprehensive high school, I had the same experience, including the ignorance of my fellow teachers about our Black pupils' histories. And the Black pupils were all put in in what were then the 'lower streams' – i.e. they were inherently stupid. And also, the same social class discrimination! I taught mainly 'lower stream' pupils and, as my treatment of them was somewhat different from how other teachers treated them, I was just about ostracised by my 'colleagues'.

For me the most significant experience was while I was on playground duty on the day the school had been celebrating 'VE Day' – that is, 'victory in Europe during WWII'. A group of white kids began to name-call the Black kids, abusing them as their parents had not contributed to this victory, so what were they doing here? Eventually a fight developed, so I had to step in and separate them. And I told myself the Black kids had to learn of their parents' contributions – 'you have to fight with knowledge, not your fists!'

So I waited for books to appear from historians. But none did. So I just had to figure out how to research at least some aspects of the history of WWII. That's what my first book was about. (Many Struggles (West Indian Workers and Service Personnel in Britain 1939-1945), Karia Press, 1985.) But while researching that, the painting of John Blanke made its appearance.

So there had been Africans in Britain way before these West Indians arrived! My mind boggled!

Where is all this history?

When Peter Fryer's book, *Staying Power* appeared, I read and read and read. I realised that so much more of the history of peoples of African (and Indian) origins/descent had to be unearthed. So that is what I have been doing since then.

Thank you John Blanke! (And Peter Fryer.)

Marika Sherwood

I imagine John Blanke as a member of the *Art Ensemble of Chicago*. He was the best dressed member of the band.

Bob and Roberta Smith
Artist

Bob and Roberta Smith (2020) *John Blanke,* 300 × 300 mm, paint on board

When John Blanke was a member of the Art Ensemble of Chicago He was the best dressed member of the Band.

I imagine John Blanke as a vivacious personality who loves to be the centre of attention, a showman – flamboyant and brilliant. He has a raucous sense of humour, a twinkle in his eye and a witty response ready on his lips. He wears excellent clothing at all times, and has an eye for quality and fine fabrics. This is partly why I wanted to create an embroidered portrait, using satin, silk thread, glass beads and lace – materials reserved for the Royal Court and noble families in John's day, so this feels appropriate. Only the best for John Blanke.

Melissa Jo Smith
Director Illuminated Arts CIC

Melissa Jo Smith (2024) *John Blanke*, 235 × 330 mm, satin, silk thread, glass beads and lace

'John Blanke – accessible through the enticing image that shows and hides so much – represents many others whose faces we cannot see'

Martin Spafford
Educator

John Blanke: an Entry Point to Enquiries About Attitudes to Race

There's an activity I've used in schools and with trainee teachers. I show them the image of John Blanke without comment, inviting their questions.

Who is he? When? What is he doing and why?

Then I show them this, by Onyeka:

The evidence suggests that Africans in Tudor society ... were integrated into their local communities in a way that many white European immigrants were not.

How can we test the truth of this historian's assertion?

We look at more evidence:
- What more we know of John Blanke: his petition for a pay rise and his royal wedding gift
- The treatment of 'other' Europeans: Catholics, Walloons, Huguenots, Romany, Hansa merchants
- Miranda Kaufmann's work on the Africans in St Botolph's parish – as well as stories such as the Black Mary Rose diver Jacques Francis
- Negative responses to Tudor Africans – from Thomas More, John Hawkins and, it seems, Queen Elizabeth

They share their findings and have to come to a conclusion: is Onyeka right?

Responses vary:
- We need more evidence
- There was a range of attitudes
- Religion, not 'race', was what defined the 'other'
- Racist attitudes existed/didn't exist
- We can't reach a final judgement based on so few examples ...

John Blanke – accessible through the enticing image that shows and hides so much – represents many others whose faces we cannot see. Witness to events at the seat of power, he is an entry point to enquiries about attitudes to 'race' before England's immersion in the triangular trade, perhaps about the impact of the Spanish Reconquista or the Reformation – but most of all, about who the working people of England really were. What we know and don't know about him and his world opens children to the power, the opportunities and the limitations of historical enquiry. And, of course, there is the excitement and astonishment on the faces of 21st century young people who see themselves in a 16th century painting and immediately rethink so much of what they have been told.

For this, he rightly features centrally in our books for the GCSE Migration course and should be a familiar face in every classroom.

Martin Spafford

For sources see page 259

I imagined John Blanke as a clarion call – his trumpet's clear, ringing sound – echoing down the millennia, uniting a past, rich in artistry, with a vision of a glorious global African future. It is a sound which will be heard by people across time and space, a sound which will summon people to come together to meet in peace and harmony rather than on the battlefield or in the mean streets. And if people want to get a bit more aggressive with each other, perhaps when QPR play Chelsea in the Champions' League Final of 3015, Blanke's trumpet will be heard like a giant referee's whistle awarding the winning penalty to the Hoops – which will be scored by our £3 billion signing from Lesotho F.C., Nelson Moshoeshoe.

In fact, seeing the image of John Blanke for the first time immediately put me in mind of the Seana Marena or 'King's Blanket' which the great southern African King Moshoeshoe I (c.1786-1870) adopted for his people, the southern Sotho, to keep them warm in his mountainous 'Kingdom of the Sky'. In centuries to come, when the salvation army of Lesotho has saved the world from alien invasion, Blanke's trumpet will be the first to break the news that the secret of King Moshoeshoe's success in battling and bamboozling the British, the Boers and the Zulus was in fact his judicious use of vibranium. At that point the truth of what many people had suspected all along will be confirmed – that Lesotho and Wakanda are one and the same.

Chris Spring
Curator, Artist and Historian

Chris Spring (2018) *John Blanke*, 257 × 350 mm, wax and wash on paper

'[W]hat could be more African than the six lions of Henry VIII's royal standard hanging from Blanke's trumpet?'

Chris Spring
Curator, Artist and Historian

John 'The King's Blanket' Blanke

Seeing the image of John Blanke for the first time immediately put me in mind of the Seana Marena or 'King's Blanket' which the great southern African King Moshoeshoe I (c.1786–1870) adopted for his people, the southern Sotho. After all, apart from John Blanke himself, what could be more African than the six lions of Henry VIII's royal standard hanging from Blanke's trumpet?

In the early nineteenth century King Moshoeshoe by turns made alliances with or fought against the British, the Boers and the Zulus to lay the foundations of what became the independent nation of Lesotho, the mountainous 'Kingdom of the Sky'. Towards the end of his life Moshoeshoe met the Scottish trader Donald Fraser and made arguably the most significant decision of the many extraordinary feats he had accomplished on behalf of his people. He ordered a consignment of blankets which Fraser had brought with him, even though a fault in the Jacquard weaving process with which they were manufactured appeared in lines running vertically down the finished product.

'Your majesty, if you order a thousand of these blankets, I will make sure that the fault lines which you see on these samples are removed,' said Fraser.

'No,' replied Moshoeshoe, 'we like the lines, we will make them our own – and we will order ten thousand of your blankets!'

Today every Sotho man or woman who wears the Seana Marena does so with the fault lines proudly displayed – and always running vertically, never horizontally. Another source of pride – to both John Blanke and to King Moshoeshoe – must surely be that the Wakandan security forces in the film *The Black Panther* all wear the Seana Marena, The King's Blanket. In its delicious blending of African languages, longstanding artistic traditions from across the continent and highly advanced 'vibranium'-driven technology, Wakanda seems to encapsulate the ideas and philosophy which constitute the phenomenon of Afrofuturism, in which John Blanke plays his part.

Chris Spring

For sources see page 259

I imagined John Blanke as a maverick. A spark in the court, a musical experimenter, respected and cherished amongst his tight coterie of peers. He'd be a loyal, funny, mischievous friend. A persuasive negotiator, he would have enjoyed and shared the fruits of his labours. A courageous and resilient human being, who knew how to see where he had landed, literally, and use his wits, charm and talent to make a successful life as a member of King Henry's household. I like to imagine he had kids; over the past six years I've been creating a series of paintings of black Elizabethans in various groupings and settings. Any one of my powerful, dignified, elegant young characters could be a child of John Blanke.

Siobhan Stanley
Artist

Siobhan Stanley (2019) *John Blanke*, 210 × 297 mm, oil on card

I imagined John Blanke not as an image, I hear him in the horns of a soul record and the deepest of Blues. If the drum was the very first instrument used when our speech was forbidden, then the trumpet is our song and it has proven everlasting when the wind sings from (that) shore to (this) shore.

SuAndi
Poet, Librettist, Live Art Practitioner

John Blanke
by SuAndi

Caught caged
And tis true
No glass to reflect
No features to compare
No language to explain
No understanding to hear
How, they will wonder

To those closest to the crown
My value reflects the worth of the treasury
The breadth of the kingdom
The power of the throne
I am no jester commanded tomfoolery
No captive savage for ladies to see and swoon
I stand shoulder to shoulder
My talent linked harmoniously
In this sextet

Though the court may wonder and be wary
I give no purpose for fear.
I am foreign yet familiar
Neither sentinel nor soldier
I carry no weapon to slay the heart
Only music to rouse the soul
In ceremonial ritual
I keep my place in pace in time
In tempo
I am melodious

I am schooled to literate
Enough to advocate advance and move forward
While my country men lay chattled
I claim my freedom though my art
The right to petition
And gain promotion by royal approval

Sometimes when trade winds blow
Alize carries the energy of my horn home
A trumpet of remembrance to those left behind
So when leaves rustle and grasses moan
I am the warrior lost,
Returned

I know this place

I am a man free in this strange land of no return
With
No glass to reflect
No features to compare
No language to explain
No understanding to hear
I will always be a wonder
Of wonderment

© SuAndi 2017

I imagined John Blanke as a graphic crowbar with which to continue to prise open, ever so slightly, the cultural door that separates us from a fuller understanding of Black British history.

Knowing where he was speaks to where we are and offers us both the vital light of context and, in turbulent times, much needed additional anchorage.

Mark Thompson
Poet

Our Tudor Rose Of Darkness
by Mark Thompson

As I look back across time
for the first in a long line
of black faces throughout history
to call these islands... home,
it seems to me I find the pages blank
(apart from a few Romans)
until I find the pages Blanke has filled.

Previous reams of white are barely broken
before these darker lines, too rarely spoken
telling us no tales at all until quite lately
of quite how greatly Blanke was skilled.

So while we know now what the man was paid,
we will never hear just how he played.
Nor will we be sure if he could blow
like Satchmo, Davis or Marsalis,
but regardless, what we do know is this,
the tunes our Tudor rose of darkness played
included climbs and falls
that scaled the very highest
of all our palace walls.

Despite the court being where it was written
I contend one could be forgiven
for thinking his was a record
some still wish would remain unheard;
unlike the man himself,
who, with regal banners unfurled
trumpeted his own worth unto the world
as he weighed well his skills in earthly wealth.

Alas, eventually he slips
without lipped fanfare from our view
but not before both in, and to
one of this land, this man was wed
his brown skinned self, not hid
by the violet gown gifted to him by the crown
(yes he rocked a purple suit
well before many a famous prince did).

But seriously, I doubt 'John Blanke' was ever more
to him, than a stage name, an ironic soubriquet
something some deemed as funny.
Perhaps this assumed nom de plume,
was found by Brits far easier to say
than the name first given to this,
our beloved Blackamoor, by his kith and kin.
Still surely all those insults would be surpassed,
if at least that name was not made to last
as to forget him, would truly be, an historic sin.
Blanke's story is a two-tone riddle,
which we see, at best, only half-drawn,
Britain's Blacke Tudor Trumpet, pictured right in
    the middle,
but clearly, of African Ancestry born.

© Mark Thompson (2017)

I imagined John Blanke as a well-respected and extremely talented musician. To be a trumpeter in the King's court, his ability had to be exceptional. He had to be a cut above other trumpeters. He would have been focused, confident and driven. I see him as inspiration, there are no boundaries and we all can make history.

Tonderai
Artist

Tonderai (2015) *John Blanke*,
210 × 297 mm, pencil on paper

I imagined John Blanke as a familiar musical icon. The Bob Marley of his time. A recognisable brown face in a sea of beige with his own signature look that no formal event could overturn. His name may have been given to him, his attire changed from country to country and court to court but his music and spirituality he would carry with him wherever he travelled. He was no stranger to royalty, formality or choreographed order – it flowed through his veins. Mediocrity was never an option, excellence was his middle name. A man of integrity he expected nothing less from others and wouldn't settle for anything less. In England he planted his seed, marrying the woman of his dreams with gifts from the King, completing another chapter of his unwritten living biography. We eagerly turned the page to learn more, but like a vibrant life short lived we are left longing and wondering what was and what would have been.

Hannah Uzor
Artist

Hannah Uzor (2024) *John Blanke*, 210 × 297 mm, charcoal and graphite on paper

'What did it feel like to look different from the majority, and to have your difference … a reminder that you lacked the heritage that powered the country's class system?'

Steven Veerapen
Historical Writer

John Blanke's Dual Lives

Writing historical fiction is – if you'll forgive the pun – all about filling in the blanks. In the case of John Blanke, there are many, which leaves much room for speculation. In considering how to include him in my upcoming series set at the early court of Henry VIII, I was drawn to the idea of liminality: of a life lived in a space between categories of race and class. John was a paid servant, and thus of higher social standing than plenty of his white contemporaries. But it doesn't follow that his life was an easy one. In early modern England, appearance was everything. A gentleman looked and dressed like a gentleman; a king looked and dressed like a king; a wicked man was hunchbacked and dark; and a wicked woman was old and crooked. If people failed to reflect outwardly what they were inwardly, society risked lapsing into disorder. What, then, did early moderns make of black people who were apt to be dressed in the respectable clothing of their English rank or in the foreign garb used to counterfeit the exotic?

It seems, in the main, that black people were treated as novelties in early modern British courts: as talking points or ornaments. Thus, whilst they might make better livings than many, they were still very much at a personal disadvantage (those who weren't given ironical names were often still defined by their colour: as 'Blakemoors' and 'Blackmoors'). They were 'strangers' – a state of being which became increasingly distrusted. Further, the period prized whiteness as a hallmark of beauty, and associated blackness (and 'sable', 'darkness', 'duskiness') with vice and ugliness. This longstanding association has been passed down to us: we still speak and write of 'black looks' and 'dark looks', and the colour white continues to be associated with virtue and purity. Certainly, there were outright racists in the period, as, unfortunately, they exist in every period. More subtle, however, was the casual and unintended racism of dressing people up and parading them as showpieces and exotic 'others'. Lucrative this must have been – but pleasant in a world which was all about fitting into distinct categories?

This is what interested me. What did it feel like to look different from the majority, and to have your difference, on the one hand, your source of prestige and, on the other, a reminder that you lacked the heritage that powered the country's class system? It seems to me that John very likely lived a dual life: in the Court, he was privileged and feted as an exotic servant; in the City, he might well have been prey to the growing discontent towards the stranger. Neither of these, I think, would have been easy to deal with. What John must have counted on to see him through was sheer strength of personality. In creatively constructing John – and his dual-heritage, fictional son, Anthony – this would be the profile by which I sought to explore the challenges and experiences of being – and facing being – different in the Henrician Court and City.

I imagine John Blanke as a young man finding expression in music. Filling the air, drawn to the trumpet's resounding call, an extension of his soul. Each note, a testament to his resilience and creativity. Each note transcends boundaries in the courts and gatherings of nobility – captivating audiences and forging connections beyond race or class.

Angela Vives
Illustrator

Angela Vives (2024) *John Blanke*, 210 × 297 mm, gouache paint on archival Fabriano paper

'Could John Blanke, change the perception of 16th century Black Britons?'

Robin Walker
Writer and Historian

A Black Man with a Trumpet: Changing Perceptions

Black men with trumpets were often icons changing perceptions of how their people were seen by outsiders. Wynton Marsalis, Dizzy Gillespie and Louis Armstrong changed scholarly perceptions of African Americans. The big question is: Could John Blanke, the trumpeter on the 1511 Westminster Tournament Roll, do something similar for 16th century Black Britons?

I have long taught that Black history professionals should marshal historical data to challenge anti-Black perceptions. Other professionals share this view. What they and I disagree upon is: Which historical stories should we prioritise to challenge anti-Black perceptions?

Some believe the CORE of Black history should be Black historical figures that appeared in European History. Black British history, for example, contains the 'Ivory Bangle Lady' from Roman times, to the likes of Olaudah Equiano, Mary Prince, William Cuffay, Ira Aldridge, Samuel Coleridge Taylor, Leslie Hutchinson and Claudia Jones.

By contrast, I believe that the CORE focus should be on Black people within pre European influenced African societies. This shows what Black people were capable of in all African settings. Furthermore, I regard all other Black history, i.e. Black figures in British, European, American and Asian history, as PERIPHERAL history. Could John Blanke, a Black man with a trumpet, change my position on this matter?

With the publication of Onyeka's exquisite *Blackamoores: Africans in Tudor England*, we learn of perhaps 350 documented Africans in Renaissance England. Many were of Moorish Iberian heritage and were people of status. John Blanke, for example, received unprecedented wedding gifts from the National Treasury. This raises questions such as: Why was he so valued? Did Blanke write the music performed by the trumpeters on the Westminster Tournament Roll?

Professor Maulana Karenga suggests that for Africans to make history, they must shape the world around them in African images and interests. Onyeka suggests the Renaissance-era Blacks accomplished this by bringing Moorish Iberian culture to England. It would be wonderful if future scholarship could document Moorish musical elements brought into England, perhaps even by Blanke himself.

Robin Walker

For sources see page 259

I imagined John Blanke as a young Spanish trumpeter of Moorish descent and culture who admired his lady Katherine of Aragon and who went to England with her entourage with a sense of trepidation, leaving behind his beloved Spain and its Moorish architecture and culture to tolerate, for him, the new ways of the English court. That he flourished is testament to his strength of character, and the undoubted respect, patronage and probable fondness of Katherine.

Barry Walmsley
Artist

Barry Walmsley (2024) *John Blanke*, 210 × 297 mm, pencil on paper

'[John Blanke's] image never fails to generate astonishment, interest, serious debate and a re-consideration of the status quo'

Tony Warner
Director of Black History Walks

John Blanke: Ammunition for the Fight Against a Prejudiced Version of the Past

John Blanke is a legend whose legacy inspires us today. The image alone has been enough to invert embedded stereotypes and explode imaginations. Whether he came from the 16th century Moorish civilisations of Spain or one of the ancient West African nation states, his presence gives us ammunition for the fight against a prejudiced version of the past. This image has been a bedrock resource on our 15 walks and numerous presentations delivered over the last 20 years. The image never fails to generate astonishment, interest, serious debate and a re-consideration of the status quo.

Tony Warner

I imagined John Blanke as Olori Orin, a Yoruba head of music, a musician and inventor of brass instruments invited to Britain to teach how these instruments are made and played. He and his family made and constructed these instruments with such skill he spent many years touring the world sharing his talents and cultures across the lands.

It's been an honour to be a part of this project, and I hope my work would make Olori Orin proud.

Kes Young
Heart in Art Creative Director

Kes Young (2020) *John Blanke*, 210 × 297 mm, mosaic art work

Artificial Intelligence and the John Blanke Project

When the Project started in 2016 artificial intelligence (AI) was a science fiction dream today the closing months of 2024 it is a reality or rather machine intelligence with generative AI a creative intelligence designing and developing new content still some way off. Nevertheless AI today as found in ChatGPT and Midjourney is capable a having intelligent conversations and producing convincing visuals respectively. It would seem natural to involve AI in reimagining John Blanke.

Conversing with AI requires so called prompting or asking conversational questions. What follows are questions Chat GPT to imagine John Blanke.

Despite multiple attempts, ChatGPT was unable to depict John Blanke playing a Baroque valveless trumpet wearing a turban. The 'valveless trumpet' is a well-documented historical instrument easily found via a simple 'valveless trumpet' Google search. Despite assurances that the image would show Blanke in a turban playing a valveless trumpet, both generated images featured a feathered cap instead of a turban and depicted him with a modern valved trumpet. This highlighted a clear misunderstanding of both historical accuracy and my prompts.

After repeated failures to correct these inaccuracies, with the suggestion and support of an artist already skilled in promoting AI for his images – Jason Lee – I moved to another AI platform designed specifically for creating images – Midjourney. With more precise prompting, I produced the more accurate representation of John Blanke with Midjourney as seen.

AI is becoming a powerful tool for exploring and rethinking the past using historical sources. However, it's not perfect yet, and human knowledge is still essential to ensure accuracy and provide deeper understanding.

Sources

Dr Toyin Agbetu

Walter Mosley I https://www.waltermosley.com/bio/ (accessed 6th December 2024)

Nalo Hopkinson https://www.nalohopkinson.com/index.html (accessed 6th December 2024)

Courttia Newland, https://en.wikipedia.org/wiki/Courttia_Newland (accessed 6th December 2024)

Albert Einstein https://www.quora.com/Albert-Einstein-reportedly-said-The-true-sign-of-intelligence-is-not-knowledge-but-imagination-What-did-he-mean(accessed 6th December 2024)

Miranda Kaufmann

John Blanke Oxford Dictionary of National Biography https://www.oxforddnb.com/display/10.1093/ref:odnb/9780198614128.001.0001/odnb-9780198614128-e-107145 (accessed 12th November 2024)

'Africans in Britain, 1500-1640'- Oxford D.Phil. thesis (2012). http://www.mirandakaufmann.com/thesis.html (accessed 12th November 2024)

Presenting the Black Past – How History Must Change the Media http://www.mirandakaufmann.com/blog/presenting-the-black-past-how-history-must-change-the-media (accessed 12th November 2024)

Robin Walker

Bibliography

Maulana Karenga, *Introduction to Black Studies*, 4th Edition, US, University of Sankore, 2010, p.66

Onyeka, *Blackamoores: Africans in Tudor England*, UK, Narrative Eye and The Circle with a Dot, 2014, p.209

Robin Walker, *The Black Musical Tradition AND Early Black Literature*, UK, Reklaw Education Limited, 2015, pp.29-32

Robin Walker, Siaf Millar & Saran Keita, *Everyday Life in an Early West African Empire*, UK, Jacinth Martin's SIVEN Publishing, 2013, pp.5-6

A longer version of Robin Walker's article with more detail is available https://www.johnblanke.com/robin-walker.html (accessed 12th November 2024)

Jan Marsh

Holbein's drawings of Tudor courtiers https://bit.ly/3O5ujUr (accessed 12th November 2024)

Dan Lyndon

Source materials for a baseline test for my year 7s http://www.blackhistory4schools.com/tudors/beginninghistory.pdf (accessed 12th November 2024)

Professor Olivette Otele

Alessandro de Medici https://en.wikipedia.org/wiki/Alessandro_de%27_Medici,_Duke_of_Florence (accessed 12th November 2024)

Juan Latino https://en.wikipedia.org/wiki/Juan_Latino (accessed 12th November 2024)

Chris Spring

The Seana Marena or 'King's Blanket https://www.britishmuseum.org/collection/object/E_2012-2018-1(accessed 12th November 2024)

King Moshoeshoe I https://www.sahistory.org.za/people/king-moshoeshoe-i (accessed 12th November 2024)

Phil Day

Select Bibliography:

Christian, David, Maps of Time (2004)

Davis, David Brion, Inhuman Bondage: The Rise and Fall of Slavery in the New World (2006)

Day, Philip, Rap History of the World (2013) http://www.raphistoryoftheworld.com/ (accessed 12th November 2024)

Day, Philip, Disease and Big History: A Dark Side of Interaction (2017) https://bighistory.org/Origins/Origins_VII_03.pdf (accessed 12th November 2024)

Kamen, Henry, Empire: How Spain Became a World Power 1492-1763 (2003)

Kaufmann M., Black Tudors: The Untold Story (2017)

McNeill, J.R., Mosquito Empires: Ecology and War in the Greater Caribbean, 1620-1914 (2010)

Jeffrey Green

13th century statue of St Maurice in Magdeburg cathedral https://www.johnblanke.com/st-maurice.html (accessed 12th November 2024)

Francis Barber Michael Bundock, *The Fortunes of Francis Barber* Yale University Press, 2015, pages 216-217

Olaudah Equiano https://rammcollections.org.uk/2020/10/01/black-history-month-portrait-of-an-african/ (accessed 12th November 2024)

Prof. Nandini Das

Adagia – Book of Proverbs
  https://en.wikipedia.org/wiki/Adagia (accessed 12th November 2024)

Desiderius Erasmus – Dutch Christian humanist scholar
  https://en.wikipedia.org/wiki/Erasmus (accessed 12th November 2024)

Lauren Johnson

The woman who removed the sheets from Catherine's marital bed – Lucy Worsley re-enacted this role in her BBC documentary *Six Wives* and featured in a tweet from @ArchivetoBlockbuster – Bringing Diversity to the BigScreen
  https://x.com/A2BFour/status/809351684568793088/photo/1

Spanish Princess series on Starz
  https://www.starz.com/us/en/series/the-spanish-princess/42457
  Dr Emma Luisa Cahill Marrón

Strabo – a Greek geographer, philosopher, and historian
  https://en.wikipedia.org/wiki/Strabo

Afro-Turks
  https://bit.ly/48NifRc

Ninya Mikhaila

British money pre decimalisation in Feb 1971
  https://en.wikipedia.org/wiki/Decimal_Day

Select Bibliography:
The King's Servants A Tudor Tailor Case Study by Caroline Johnson
  Editors: Jane Malcolm-Davies & Ninya Mikhaila
  https://www.tudortailor.com/the-kings-servants

Sean Cunningham

John Blanke's petition for increased wages in 1512,
  https://manyheadedmonster.com/2015/07/27/john-blanke-henry-viiis-black-trumpeter-petitions-for-a-back-dated-pay-increase-2/

Renée Landell

2022 report by the Living Wage Foundation
  https://www.livingwage.org.uk/employee-jobs-below-real-living-wage-2022

John Blanke's petition for increased wages in 1512,
  https://manyheadedmonster.com/2015/07/27/john-blanke-henry-viiis-black-trumpeter-petitions-for-a-back-dated-pay-increase-2/

Jeff Bowersox

The Black advisors, guards, and servants who populated the Hohenstaufen court in the 12th and 13th centuries
  https://blackcentraleurope.com/sources/1000-1500/

Kendall Francis

Portrait of an African Man (Christophle le more?) c.1525
  https://www.rijksmuseum.nl/en/collection/SK-A-4986/catalogue-entry

Portrait of a Wealthy African c.1530
  https://fleurtyherald.wordpress.com/wp-content/uploads/2017/11/portrait-of-a-wealthy-african.jpg

Portrait of an unknown African woman holding a clock c.1580
  https://fashionhistory.fitnyc.edu/1583-5-carracci-african-woman-clock/

Martin Spafford

The Black Mary Rose diver Jacques Francis
  http://www.mirandakaufmann.com/bbc-history-magazine.html

Spanish Reconquista
  https://en.wikipedia.org/wiki/Reconquista

The Reformation
  https://en.wikipedia.org/wiki/Reformation

Our books for the GCSE Migration course
  https://www.hoddereducation.com/history/ocr-gcse-history-shp-migrants-to-britain-c-1250-to-present

Recommended reading

Books

Anglo, S. (1968) *The Great Tournament Roll of Westminster*, Clarendon Press, Oxford

Habib, I. (2007) *Black Lives in the English Archives, 1500-1677: Imprints of the Invisible*, Routledge

Kaufmann, M. (2017) *Black Tudors: The Untold Story*, Oneworld, London

Onyeka, (Oct 2013) *Blackamoores: Africans in Tudor England, Their Presence*,

van Pelt, N.T. (2023) *Intercultural Explorations and the Court of Henry VIII*. Oxford Textual Perspectives. Oxford: Oxford University Press

Articles and Chapters

John Blanke Oxford Dictionary of National Biography entry https://www.oxforddnb.com/view/10.1093/ref:odnb/9780198614128.001.0001/odnb-9780198614128-e-107145

Ohajuru, M.I. (2024) *John Blanke: The Black Trumpet* in Bradshaw, P. (ed) *Beyond the Bassline: 500 Years of Black British Music*, London, British Library, pp. 42-44

Ohajuru, M.I. (2022) *Insights into John Blanke's Image from The John Blanke Project*, in Bolland, C. (ed) *The Tudors: Passion, Power and Politics*, London, National Portrait Gallery, pp. 28-30

Ohajuru, M.I. (2020) *Before and After the Eighteenth Century: The John Blanke Project* in Grezina, H. G. (ed) *Britain's Black Past* Liverpool, Liverpool University Press, pp. 7-25

Twycross, M. (2023) *John Blanke's Hat and its Contexts. Part 1: Turbans and Islamic Dress at the Court of Henry VIII*. Medieval English Theatre, 45, pp. 1–65.

van Pelt, N.T. (2022) *John Blanke's Wages: No Business Like Show Business*. Medieval English Theatre, 44, pp. 3–35.

Online Short Course

Black Tudors: The Untold Story
Discover the little-known history of Black Africans in Tudor England and challenge your preconceptions of Black history. https://www.futurelearn.com/courses/black-tudors

John Blanke Clothing

The Tudor Tailor's Books
The King's Servants
A Tudor Tailor Case Study by Caroline Johnson
Editors: Jane Malcolm-Davies & Ninya Mikhaila
The Typical Tudor
Reconstructing Everyday 16th Century Dress

Exhibition Catalogues

The Metropolitan Museum, New York, USA
Cleland, E. & Eaker, A (2022) *The Tudors: Art and Majesty in Renaissance England*, New York, The Met,

Walters Art Museum, Baltimore, USA
Janeath Spicer ed.(2012) *Revealing the African Presence in Renaissance Europe*. Baltimore: Walters Art Museum, (available free to download online. http://bit.ly/IBLG_Spicer)

Walker Art Gallery, Liverpool, UK
Bolland, C. (ed) *The Tudors: Passion, Power and Politics*, London, National Portrait Gallery

British Museum
Bate, J. and D. Thornton (2012) *Shakespeare: Staging the World* London/Oxford University Press New York

British Library
Bradshaw, P. (ed) (2024) *Beyond the Bassline : 500 Years of Black British Music* British Library

John Blanke Live!

The John Blanke Project in the form of a workshop – John Blanke Live! – has been taken into prison and the schoolroom to inspire and encourage.

A typical John Blanke Project Live! workshop is in four parts over two and half hours:

Part 1 Presentation – John Blanke
An introduction to the Black presence in Renaissance Europe through the history of John Blanke and his image compared to the images of the Black St Maurice and the Black Magus or king from the Adoration scene.

Part 2 Presentation – The Project
The John Blanke project is introduced as a multidisciplinary venture of art, music and poetry

Part 3 Participation
Participants are invited to draw John Blanke as they imagined he might look using pencil or charcoal on a piece of A4 paper, finishing by writing a sentence beginning with the statement I imagined John Blanke as…

Part 4 Symposium
Each member of the workshop presents their imagined John Blanke to the rest of the group.

Examples from John Blanke Project Live! workshops are given on the following pages.

These images were created by eight and nine-year-old school children during workshops inspired by the story of John Blanke. Their work reflects their creativity and engagement with history. These images are included here with respect and admiration for their work, and no identifying details have been used to maintain the children's privacy.

I imagined John Blanke as enjoying playing the trumpet. Not proud or showing off but happy making a beautiful sound.

I imagine John Blanke as my music teacher.

I see him as posh, polite gentleman who helped King Henry gain is posision (sic)

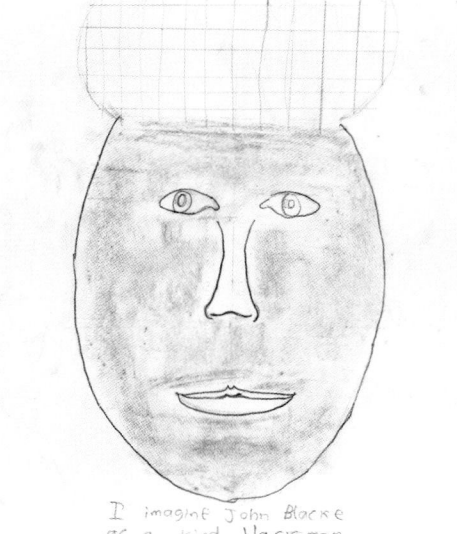

I imagine John Blanke as kind Blackman that is strong because he can lift a heavy trumpet.

I imagine John Blanke as a handsome young man.

I imagine John Blanke as a respectful loyal person who loves music.

I imagine that John Blane was a young, proud man letting people know when the king arrived and when he left. I believe he also tried to show his talent to the people and the king.

The John Blanke Project Timeline

			Artists	Historians
	Commissioned first artist Stephen B. Whatley to re-imagine John Blanke	2015	1	
	Commissioned first historian Miranda Kaufmann to re-imagine John Blanke	2016	5	2
	JohnBlanke.com live			
📺	Featured in *Black and British: A Forgotten History* with David Olusoga on BBC2			
JOHN BLANKE	BBC plaque to John Blanke at Greenwich Old Naval College visitors centre			
	First John Blanke Project Live! School Workshop Whittingham Primary	2017	30	10
	First Symposium: British Library			
	First senior citizens' workshop with Caribbean Social Forum	2018	40	19
	Workshop in Pentonville Prison	2019	45	23
	First international workshop in L'Esterre RC Primary School in L'Esterre, Carricou Grenada	2020	55	27
📺	Alison Hammond: Back to School on ITV			
🏰	Take over Historic Royal Palaces Hampton Court twitter account for the day			
📚	Chapter on the Project in *Britain's Black Past* edited by Gretchen H Gerzina published by Liverpool University Press			
📺	*Black Classical Music: The Forgotten History* with Lenny Henry on BBC 2			
JOHN BLANKE	Nubian Jaq blue plaque for John Blanke at Trinity Laban Conservatoire, Greenwich	2021	57	28
Walker Art Gallery	Exhibition at Liverpool Walker Art Gallery	2022	60	30
📚	Essay in *The Tudors: Passion, Power and Politics* edited by Charlotte Bolland published by National Portrait Gallery			
THE NATIONAL ARCHIVES / THE MET / NPG	Featured in The National Archive Collection Presented at The Metropolitan Museum, New York Featured in the new hang of the National Portrait Gallery Presentation at San Francisco Fine Art Museum	2023	72	32
	Crowdsourced funding for book of the project Paul Mellon Publication Fund donation	2024	80	35
📚	Published book of Project	2025	80	35

Crowdfunder Thanks

Below there is a listing of the folk who through the generosity of their crowdfunded donations helped publish this book.

Publishing the Book of The John Blanke Project

https://www.crowdfunder.co.uk/p/publishing-the-book-of-the-john-blanke-project

Crowdsourcing is not a new way of publishing. In the 18th century it was called 'publishing by subscription', today it is 'crowdfunding'. Subscription at the time was not common, it was reserved for books of specialist subjects. One such subject funded by subscription was autobiographical accounts of the enslaved – slave narratives. For example, Olaudah Equiano, freed slave, writer and abolitionist, published the first edition of *The Interesting Narrative of the Life of Olaudah Equiano, Or Gustavus Vassa, The African*, in 1789 and had over 300 subscribers. These were led by the Prince of Wales and the Duke of York, as well as leading abolitionists Thomas Clarkson and Granville Sharp.. I believe the John Blanke Project Book crowdfunders aka subscribers described below are following in that 18th century practice.

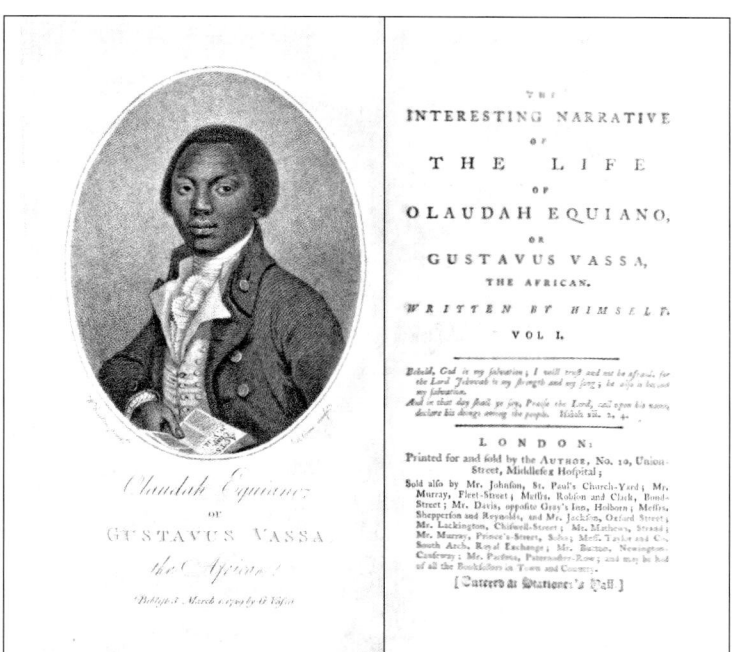

Published by Subscription 1789. Courtesy of the John Carter Brown Library.

I wish to thank the following crowdfunders aka subscribers to the Book of the John Blanke Project:

Sandra Agard · Sanchia Alasia · Joanne Anderson · SuAndi · Margaret T. Andrews · Grant Bage · Elaine Baldry · Mandy Banton · Elizabeth Barrett · Gaverne Bennett · Brian Bennett · Adam Benzan · Carla Benzan · Peter Bowden · Jeff Bowersox · Yvonne Boyle · Dr Emily Bradfield · Paul Bradshaw · Agenda Brown · Margaret Busby · Sam Bushell · Charles Card-Reynolds · David Cobley · Sylvia Collicott · Lynn Collie · Fiona Collins · Deborah Conway-Read · Patrick Craig · Elizabeth Crosby · Lynda Culley · Ebun Culwin · Ann Danks · Subhadra Das · Susan Deans-Smith · Liam Devlin · Alison Donnell · Tricia and Dave Douglas · Ashley Downing · Janet Dugdale · Amy Dunn · Lucie Dutton · Nasra Elliott · Cathy FitzGerald · Catherine Fletcher · Sharon Foster · Carmen Fracchia · Michelle Lisa Gayle · Sarah Gee · Gretchen Gerzina · Ms B S Z Grant · Marian Gwyn · Jane Hamer · Jenny Head · Pavel and Sylva Hlousek · Elaine Huggett · Bill Hunt · Janine Irons · Lucy James · Catherine Johnson · Claudette Johnson · Howard Jones · Ellen Kray and Burkhard Acktun · Maria del Pilar Kaladeen · Miranda Kaufmann · Victoria Lane · Art Historical London · Dr Stephen Longstaffe · Judith and Bob McAra · Seema McArdle · Peter McCaldon · Carl McFarlane · John and Krys McKay · Jim McLaughlin and Anne Marie Martin · Marie-Anne McQuay · Liz Millman · Margaret Monod · Andrea Montgomery · Kate Morrison · Wade Newell-Stephenson · Ormond and Kate Noonan · Alisha O'Brien-Coker · Kate O'Donoghue · Peter O'Donoghue · Ben Ohajuru · Daveena Ogene · Olivette Otele · Thomas Padula · Mark Palframan · Martin Plaut · Laura Popoviciu · Dorothy Price · Leslie Primo · Nicole Pritchard · Christopher Rabson · Ellen Rawson · Anna Redding · Mark Rickards · Ignatius Sancho · David Santiuste · Shasta Schatz · Jo Sealy · Richard Shaw · John Siblon · Richard Smith · Richard Stemp · Dave and Denise Street · Bolanle Tajudeen · Leah Thorn · Anthony Toner · Mark Tricker · Philip Tucker · Tina Vadaneaux · Cheryl Vidal · Angela Vives · Ingrid M. Wallenborg · Diane Ward · Steve and Gaynor Waring · Eesha Waseem · Gladys West · Leah West · Phil Woodford · Vanessa Woolf · Barbara Wright · Rachel Wright · Megan Zander

I would like to extend my gratitude to all those subscribers who, while preferring to remain anonymous, have equally contributed to making the book's publication possible.

With thanks and gratitude to both named and anonymous crowdfunders.

Michael I. Ohajuru

Acknowledgements

The very first thing I want to do is thank the artists and historians who accepted my invitation to imagine John Blanke. Without their open-mindedness, vision, intellect, and imagination, there would be no John Blanke Project. I am often asked, 'Which is your favourite contribution?' To borrow the sentiment of an Arabic proverb: 'People are equal, like the teeth of a comb.' Each contribution holds its own unique value, just as every tooth in a comb is essential to its purpose. I love them all for that very reason, and to every artist and historian involved, I offer my heartfelt thanks.

I am eternally grateful to Cherry Warren for introducing me to Renaissance art and sparking my love for 16th century Florentine masterpieces. Artists like Botticelli, Ghirlandaio, Leonardo, and Michelangelo remain benchmarks of true art for me. Her early guidance shaped my artistic journey. During my Art History degree at the Open University, my love for Renaissance art deepened academically, a passion that remains with me to this day. I particularly thank my OU tutors, including Professor Clare Taylor and the late Professor Charles Harrison – his writings and videos remain foundational to my art history practice. Special thanks also to my 2007 OU Arts summer school friends, Emily Bradfield and Lynda Culley, who remain art-loving and supportive friends.

Many institutions and organisations have supported me and the project, and I thank them elsewhere in this book. However, I would like to name a few individuals for their specific contributions: Professor Philip Murphy and Professor Kingsley Abbott at the Institute of Commonwealth Studies, who provided me with an academic home to continue my research into the Black presence in Renaissance Europe; Peter O'Donoghue at the College of Arms, a steadfast supporter from the Project's inception; Charlotte Bolland at the National Portrait Gallery; Kathy Donoghue and Lucy Johnson at National Museums Liverpool; and Denise Murrell at The Met: Jonah Albert, Dr Aleema Gray and Dr Mykaell Riley at the British Museum whose encouragement and curatorial guidance has been invaluable. I greatly appreciate the continued efforts and support of Martin Hickman and Gaby Monteiro at Canbury Press who spurred me on to bring the book to life.

I also owe thanks to art historians and curators who helped me bring John Blanke and the Project to life: Professor Gretchen Gerzina, Dr Kathy Chater, Professor Carmen Fracchia, Alisha O'Brien-Coker, and Tara Munroe. My friends at the Stanley Spencer Gallery in Cookham encouraged my art history practice and deepened my love for portraiture. Spencer's pencil on paper portraits are the artistic foundation of this project.

The media has played a great role in the project's success. My thanks to Paul Bradshaw at *Viral Histories*, Kofi Kusitor at Colourful Radio, and Fred Kudjo Kuwornu for featuring John Blanke in *We Are Here*.

Finally, I am profoundly grateful to my family and friends whose love and support have sustained me. Special thanks to Jim McLaughlin, Dave Street, Bob McCara, and the late Pam Dodd for their moral support and good humour.

I would like to close by highlighting two individuals without whom this project would not exist. Dr Miranda Kaufmann, my dear friend and colleague, introduced me to John Blanke's historical significance and has been a constant and enthusiastic supporter. Her scholarship on the Black presence in Tudor England has been a cornerstone of the project.

The second is my partner, Ebun Culwin, whose contribution of the John Blanke facsimile on vellum brought the project to life in a profound way. Ebun's unconditional love and support have been my anchor throughout this journey. Words cannot express my gratitude.

To all who have been part of this journey, thank you.

Michael I. Ohajuru
Friday 24 January 2025

Corporate and institution thanks

The John Blanke Project is and has been helped by the following institutions. In no particular order, I would like to acknowledge that help.

College of Arms
National Trust Sutton House
British Library
The National Archives
Royal Army Corps Band
Institute of Commonwealth Studies
What's Happening in Black British History?
BBC
Caribbean Social Forum
Black History Walks
Viral History
Ed Cross Fine Art Limited
the blackShed Gallery
Beardsmore Gallery
Unison's Hammersmith and Fulham Black Members' Group
Lion TV
The University of Edinburgh Student Experience Grants
ITV
Walker Art Gallery
National Portrait Gallery
Douglas Road Productions
Historic Royal Palaces
The Metropolitan Museum, New York
Shade Podcast
Colourful Radio
Enrich Learning

The John Blanke Project Instructional Thanks Page
https://www.johnblanke.com/thanks.html

The John Blanke Project in videos and podcasts

Videos

School of Advanced Studies, University of London What's Happening in Black British History April 2016
The John Blanke Project
https://youtu.be/NjXGxnkZDeg?si=KJ5GLhVXGIPKXw2v

Viral History October 2018
Who Was John Blanke? Celebrating this Black Tudor, & ways of interpreting historical figures
https://youtu.be/lbmfAz_BafY?si=yYUphbV3ctbnRzhE

School of Advanced Studies, University of London Gerald Aylmer Seminar, September 2021
Recovering Ephemeral Histories from the Archives: The John Blanke Project
https://youtu.be/DoSjh8oIf8s?si=UoFqCBUA4z5wA0pq

ITV News January 2022
John Blanke (trumpeter to two Tudor kings) gets a blue plaque (UK)
https://youtu.be/agi17qJKOwY?si=-F2rDz4sWrwwoQfk

National Museums Liverpool Exhibition 21 May 2022— 29 Aug 2022
Who is John Blanke? | Tudors: Passion Power and Politics
https://youtu.be/G2Sg-4siq_Q?si=1iAP4xhylSxr_T0n

The Metropolitan Museum, New York, January 2023
The Black Presence in Tudor England
https://youtu.be/Ng79KM6F0cA?si=lkUPuAy_TmSE_jS5

The National Archives, London April 2023
Filling in the Blankes: The Life of a Black Tudor
https://youtu.be/Oj7X0Hve4DQ?si=o_3rswhaY0u8NWj2

National Portrait Gallery, London June 2023
Who was John Blanke?
https://youtu.be/fCm6Fx2cwAs?si=2al_3RFpjGawmE7u

Sky Arts TV Jul 2023
John Blanke Project at the National Portrait Gallery
https://youtu.be/qiEdChBXxcw?si=25-tr2h5-lvj5oN6

Podcasts

Talking Tudors Podcast Episode 143, January 2022
The John Blanke Project with Michael Ohajuru
https://youtu.be/-9DDxvboXhQ?si=Oa070RG5ntvpOIwR

Not Just Tudors Episode 265, October 2023
Black Tudors: John Blanke
https://shows.acast.com/not-just-the-tudors/episodes/black-tudors

The BP2 Podcast Episode 5 November 2021 John Blanke The Great Tournament Roll of Westminster
https://podcasters.spotify.com/pod/show/the-bp2-podcast/episodes/The-BP2-Podcast-Episode-5-John-Blanke-The-Great-Tournament-Roll-of-Westminster-1511-e1adc1m/a-a6trfic

Shade (2024) Conversations with Art Visionaries April 2024 *Michael Ohajuru: In conversation with Lou Mensah*
https://pod.link/1469562537/episode/fedc5153e985416728 8e50df44634f43

Contributors

			Page
Larry Achiampong	Artist	A seasoned traveller	26
Prof Hakim Adi	Historian	John Blanke: an agent of change	28
Sandra A. Agard	Storyteller	A confident, assured Black man	30
John Agard	Artist	Not backward in coming forward	32
Dr Toyin Agbetu	Educator	Corrects and projects a more complete history of African people in the UK's past	34
Hassan Aliyu	Artist	An enchanting figure who transcends history and the boundaries of reality and legend	36
Sydney Anglo	Historian	The only black trumpeter mentioned by Heron must be the only black trumpeter depicted in the Great Tournament Roll	38
Year 9 student at Kings Priory School, North Shields	Artist	An individual who took pride in his musical role	42
Toby Laurent Belson	Artist	An international sound pioneer	44
David Bindman	Historian	John Blanke the black trumpet	46
Hazel Blue	Artist	An intelligent, ambitious soul	48
Phoebe Boswell	Artist	Shabaka Hutchings	50
Stephen Bourne	Historian	A massive jigsaw puzzle	52
Nathan Bowen	Artist	A strong-minded individual	54
Jeff Bowersox	Historian	John Blanke's legacy: unveiling the long history of the Black presence in England and Germany	56
Joanna Brown	Artist	A majestic musician	58
Victoria Burgher	Artist	An incredibly talented, dedicated musician	60
Chila Kumari Burman	Artist	An exceptional musician/trumpeter	62
Jody Burton	Artist	Someone who strived to use his skills to succeed	64
Rohan Clarke	Artist	A reflection of myself	66
Matthew Collings	Artist	A small delicate guy living in barracks	68
Ebun Culwin	Artist	A fellow diaspora musician and parent	70
Sean Cunningham	Historian	Are the 1507 John Blanke (sic) Trumpeter and 1488 John Blank (sic) Footman one and the same person ?	72
Adelaide Damoah	Artist	The firstborn son of Nana Damoah	74
Jon Daniel	Artist	A 'trump card'	76
Nandini Das	Historian	Henry's trumpeter, whose black face refuses to be washed out of history	78
Paul Dash	Artist	A survivor	80
Phil Day	Rapper	Representing themes of the highest importance in world history: interaction and connectivity	82
Phil Day	Historian	John Blanke: Illustrative of Europe's expanding connectivity	84
Kimathi Donkor	Artist	Having a strong sense of determination	86
J Draper	Historian	The first Black person In British history with a name and a portrait	88
Mengistu Etim	Artist	A talented career musician	90
Graeme Mortimer Evelyn	Artist	A powerful force of sound	92
Tinuke Fagborun	Artist	A musical prodigy	94
Dan Farrimond	Artist	A cheerful fellow	96
Jenny Fay	Artist	A thoughtful and insightful musician	98

Catherine Fletcher	Historian	John Blanke: the Tudor Roman connection?	100
Sharon Foster	Artist	A strong, charismatic, creative, black man	102
Fowokan	Artist	The man who blew a medieval fanfare that echoed down through to the 20th century	104
Brian Francis	Artist	A man who might have felt he was strange	106
Kendall Francis	Historian	Portrait of an unknown Black Man?	108
Kadija George	Poet	A talented, proud yet sad man	110
Holly Graham	Artist	A confident and assertive character	112
Jeffrey Green	Historian	John Blanke an intriguing challenge to Historians	114
Joy Gregory	Artist	The trumpeter at work with his colleagues	116
Annis Harrison	Artist	A very talented musician	118
Valda Jackson	Artist	A man of courage	120
Lauren Johnson	Historian	John Blanke had a female contemporary at the Tudor court	122
Tam Joseph	Artist	A talented man in his own right	124
Linett Kamala	Artist	A courageous and resilient creative	126
Paul Kaplan	Historian	John Blanke and his Afro-European namesakes	128
Dr Miranda Kaufmann	Historian	John Blanke – A Black Tudor	22
Kofi	Artist	A learned man	130
Atta Kwami	Artist	An adept trumpeter	132
Wole Lagunju	Artist	An aristocrat	134
Renée Landell	Researher	John Blanke's tenacity is shared among many Black Brits fighting for equitable pay and other workers' rights today	136
Vicky Lane	Curator	John Blanke: taking a portrait out of Henry VIII's Roll	138
Dee Lawrence	Artist	His family as commissioning a yard of cloth for his travels	140
Jason Lee	Artist	A prominent person within the Royal pageantry	142
Serena Lee	Historian	An adorned Black trumpeter encapsulated in posterity	144
Dave Lewis	Photographer	anything I wanted him to be	146
Joe Lillington	Artist	A man who was proud and confident in his profession	148
Prof Kate Lowe	Historian	John Blanke and acceptance of difference	150
Dan Lyndon	Historian	John Blanke Was My Gateway Drug to Black British History	152
Seema Manchanda	Artist	Physically and emotionally strong	154
Janet Manning	Artist	A lone black person in the white context of the Royal Court	156
Dr Emma Luisa Cahill Marrón	Historian	Were Juan de Salonia and John Blanke the same trumpeter?	158
Jan Marsh	Historian	An invaluable Tudor portrait	160
Maya Martin	Artist	A compelling man	162
S.I. Martin	Historian	The Blanke Slate	164
Randolph Matthews	Artist	A real person not fragmented to fit a box	166
Seema McArdle	Writer	John Blanke: representation matters	168
Pete McCaldon	Artist	A musician, then as now with a clear sense of his own worth	170
Alex McKenzie	Artist	Being from a wealthy family somewhere like modern day Mali	172
Pen Mendonça	Artist	A complex man full of character and emotion	174
Roy Merchant	Poet	One of my ancestors	176

Ninya Mikhalia	Historical Costumier	What did John Blanke's wedding clothes look like?	178
Andrea Montgomery	Playwright	A musician and storyteller	182
Sheba Montserrat	Poet	A musician, who follows his heart and art	184
Kate Morrison	Writer	A very confident, talented musician	186
Angeline Morrison	Artist	An impressive, glamorous, flamboyant and intensely talented presence	188
Avril Nanton	Tour Guide	A tour guide's view of John Blanke	190
Lawrence Narhkom	Artist	A man with great discipline, commitment and absolute professionalism	192
Jess Nash	Artist	Someone with not only talent but a deep adoration for the instrument	194
Elaine Nason	Artist	Musing on the happenings in his life	196
David Neita	Artist	A bold and brassy leader of social change	198
Ormond Noonan	Artist	A figure of intrigue and prominence	200
Dr Temi Odumosu	Historian	Marked	202
Valentine Ogunba	Rapper	An unknown figure of history	204
Adèle Oliver	Writer	John Blanke: brass in the belly of the beast	206
Onyeka	Historian	Understanding the context of John Blanke	208
Prof Olivette Otele	Historian	John Blanke, an Afro-European	210
Eugene Palmer	Artist	An individual in possession of exceptional talents	212
Brandon Pilcher	Artist	An adventurous musician	214
Keith Piper	Artist	A time traveller, a temporal, as well as geographical 'advanced guard'	216
Jane Porter	Artist	A strong, talented and unique individual	218
Dr Mary Rambaran-Olm	Artist	A cultural bridge	220
Jeremy Salmon	Artist	A quiet, humble and obviously very talented man	222
Marika Sherwood	Historian	Depiction of a Negro	224
Bob & Roberta Smith	Artist	A member of the Art Ensemble of Chicago	226
Melissa Jo Smith	Artist	A vivacious personality	228
Martin Spafford	Historian	John Blanke: an entry point to enquiries about attitudes to race	230
Chris Spring	Artist	A clarion call	232
Chris Spring	Historian	John 'The King's Blanket' Blanke	234
Siobhan Stanley	Artist	A maverick	236
SuAndi	Poet	Not as an image, I hear him in the horns of a soul record and the deepest of Blues	238
Mark Thompson	Poet	A graphic crowbar	240
Tonderai	Artist	A well-respected and extremely talented musician	242
Hannah Uzor	Artist	A familiar musical icon	244
Steven Veerapen	Writer	John Blanke's dual lives	246
Angela Vives	Artist	A young man finding expression in music	248
Robin Walker	Historian	A Black man with a trumpet: changing perceptions	250
Barry Walmsley	Artist	A young Spanish trumpeter of Moorish descent and culture	252
Tony Warner	Tour Guide	John Blanke: ammunition for the fight against a prejudiced version of the past	254
Stephen B Whatley	Artist	Olori Orin a Yoruba head of music	24
Kes Young	Artist	Both self-assured and soulful	256

Endpapers

The Great 1511 Tournament Roll of Westminster
12th and 13th February 1511

The Roll shows three main parts of the tournament. First (membranes 2-23) is the grand entrance, where a procession with John Blanke in the troop of trumpeters (membrane 4), including four knight challengers, arrives at the tilting field. Next (membranes 24-27), we see the jousting itself, with the challengers on one side, the answerers on the other, and King Henry VIII competing while Queen Katherine and the court watch from an elegant viewing gallery. Finally (membranes 27-35), the procession with John Blanke seen in the leading troop of trumpeters (membrane 28), heads back after the day's jousting. The Roll starts (membrane 1) with a heraldic symbol and ends (membrane 36) with another emblem and five verses praising Henry VIII includes the lines below.

In harry the viij owr Joye and our delyte
Subdewer of wronges mayntenar of rightwysnes

In Henry VIII, our joy and delight
Subduer of wrongs, maintainer of righteousness.

Source: Anglo, Sydney (1968). *The Great Tournament Roll of Westminster: Historical Introduction*. Oxford: Clarendon Press.

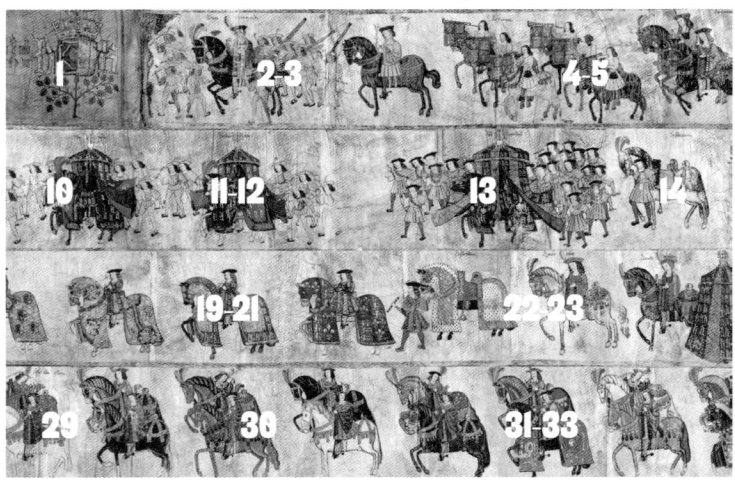

Possibly from the workshop of Thomas Wriothesley, the Garter King of Arms (1511). The Great Tournament Roll of Westminster, held at The College of Arms, London